HUMANIZING
CHILD CUSTODY DISPUTES

ABOUT THE AUTHORS

Gordon B. Plumb, Ph. D. is a practicing clinical psychologist in Carbondale, Illinois. He is founder and president of Psychological Services and Chronic Pain Management, Inc. He has been performing his unique form of custody evaluations in Southern Illinois since 1977. In the mid 1980s Dr. Plumb began teaming up with Mary Lindley on numerous court-appointed child custody cases. Out of this relationship sprang the ideas and motivation for this timely book. Dr. Plumb is a humanist, primarily trained in transactional analysis and Gestalt therapy.

Mary E. Lindley, M.S.W., C.S.W., is a board certified diplomate in clinical social work. She has earned inclusion in the NASW Register of Clinical Social Workers and is a certified child welfare specialist with the Department of Children and Family Services in Harrisburg, Illinois. She is author of *A Manual on Investigating Child Custody Reports*, published by Charles C Thomas, Publisher in 1988. Until recently she performed all court-appointed custody investigations for a seven county area in Southern Illinois.

HUMANIZING CHILD CUSTODY DISPUTES

The Family's Team

By

GORDON B. PLUMB, PH.D.

*Psychological Services and Chronic
Pain Management, Inc.*

MARY E. LINDLEY, M.S.W., C.S.W.

*Board Certified Diplomate in Clinical Social Work
NASW Register of Clinical Social Workers
Child Welfare Specialist with Illinois Department
of Children and Family Services*

Foreword by

Glenn Poshard

*Congressman
U.S. House of Representatives
Former Illinois State Senator*

CHARLES C THOMAS • PUBLISHER
Springfield • Illinois • U.S.A.

Published and Distributed Throughout the World by
CHARLES C THOMAS • PUBLISHER
2600 South First Street
Springfield, Illinois 62794-9265

This book is protected by copyright. No part of
it may be reproduced in any manner without
written permission from the publisher.

© *1990 by* CHARLES C THOMAS • PUBLISHER
ISBN 0-398-05663-3
Library of Congress Catalog Card Number: 89-20617

With THOMAS BOOKS *careful attention is given to all details of manufacturing and design. It is the Publisher's desire to present books that are satisfactory as to their physical qualities and artistic possibilities and appropriate for their particular use.* THOMAS BOOKS *will be true to those laws of quality that assure a good name and good will.*

Printed in the United States of America
SC-R-3

Library of Congress Cataloging-in-Publication Data
Plumb, Gordon B.
   Humanizing child custody disputes : the family's team / by Gordon B. Plumb, Mary E. Lindley ; foreword by Glenn Poshard.
     p. cm.
   Includes bibliographical references.
   ISBN 0-398-05663-3
   1. Family social work. 2. Family assessment. 3. Custody of children. I. Lindley, Mary E. II. Title.
HV697.P58 · 1990
362.7'1—dc20   89-20617
                                                                                CIP

FOREWORD

Children are important. That is the simple, straightforward message of this book.

All of us would like to see children grow up in a home where their physical, spiritual, and psychological security is nourished and protected. The reality of family life in America, however, is that too many children are denied that security through the break-up of the family unit. Divorce is a fact of life.

What if we could develop a process in the case of divorce proceedings, which, instead of allowing the parents to control and manipulate the children in their own selfish desires to "win" against the other parent, would help both parents better understand the needs of their children and help the court render the best possible decision on the children's future. What if we could develop a process where children are also the "winners," at least able to secure the best chance for a stable emotional future. That process has been developed. It is what this book is all about.

It is not a complicated process. It's not even expensive when compared to the emotional and psychological costs of the current adversarial process in most divorce proceedings. While I am not always in full agreement with some of the criteria, the process of custody settlement in this book is, above everything else, basic common sense. It advocates a team approach involving a social worker, a psychologist, and a family attorney working with the parties to the divorce in serving their children's emotional and psychological health.

I have been a professional educator and now legislator for the past twenty years. I have worked with thousands of children. I know that children need the same love and protection the rest of us need. Many of my former students are now functioning as "at risk" adults because they were never able to overcome the abuse they suffered as children during a divorce proceeding. I wish they had been able to avail themselves of the opportunity many more children may have when this approach becomes the rule rather than the exception.

The team approach works. It can literally save our children's lives. It should be implemented in every divorce proceeding in the country.

U.S. Congressman GLENN POSHARD

PREFACE

Throughout the text the terms "litigant" and "parents" are used to denote those who are attempting to obtain custody of children. We acknowledge that biological parents are not the only people who initiate custody litigation. Often grandparents, stepparents, other relatives, and others are intimately involved in such proceedings. We use the terms "parents" and "litigants" synonymously throughout the text for the purpose of consistency and simplicity.

At times throughout the text the authors use the personal pronouns, "I" and "we" when referring to themselves as individuals or as a team. Generally, "I" in all chapters other than Chapter V refers to the senior author.

ACKNOWLEDGMENTS

The completion of this book gives me great cause for celebration. I have many valued friends, colleagues, family, and supporters who deserve our heartfelt thanks.

First of all, my thanks to many of the judges and attorneys in Southern Illinois who have called upon us and demanded quality custody work. They have provided and continue to provide us with the experience and trust out of which came this manuscript.

Cathy Mikrut, the primary typist and patient reader for her painstaking work especially in the early stages of the manuscript.

Dr. James Peterson for his constant praise and reassurance that what I had to say was important and needed.

Jane Ross, for her after-hour efforts to get the final draft completed.

Denise Wallis, for her superior efforts in editing, time after time, the body of the manuscript and for her insightful comments on style and clarity.

Monika, Daelia, and Kathara Plumb for their enthusiastic support and obvious pride in their spouse and father.

Emily Ruppert, for her potent training and treatment during my early clinical years and for finally "making" me realize that I was O.K. and smart.

Joseph Gauld, founder of Hyde School in Bath, Maine, for his undaunted belief in me as an adolescent when most others had given up.

My grateful thanks to Congressman Glenn Poshard, Illinois, for his support and writing of the Foreword for this book and especially for his efforts in the nation's capital to initiate legislation to rid our country of the barbaric practice of contemporary custody litigation.

Finally, I want to acknowledge my family of origin: Ernest Plumb, my father, for showing me by example that meaningful accomplishments are accomplished through hard work; the memory of my mother, Peggy, who loved me unconditionally and always encouraged me to go after what I wanted; my sister, Jackie, who taught me a lot about generosity; and my brother, Les, who was a tough act to follow and a great yardstick to measure myself by.

Gordon Plumb

ACKNOWLEDGMENTS

In reflecting on my genuine enthusiasm and interest in conducting court ordered custody investigations, I am grateful to all attorneys and judges whose recommendations resulted in investigations being ordered in contested custody cases. There are numerous attorneys and judges with whom I have been associated professionally in the many custody cases in which I have been involved in approximately fourteen counties. It is, therefore, not possible to list each attorney and judge individually. I would, however, like to express my appreciation to Judge William Lewis, Chief Judge of the First Judicial Circuit in Illinois; Judge Terrence Hopkins, Chief Judge of the Second Judicial Circuit in Illinois; and to all the other judges and attorneys of both circuits. I want to especially acknowledge Judge Michael J. Henshaw and Judge Arlie Boswell, Jr. from Saline County who have provided numerous court orders resulting in my obtaining valuable experience in completing custody reports for the court. I will always be deeply indebted to Judge Henshaw and Judge Boswell for their philosophy of believing custody reports can provide beneficial assistance to them in their rendering such important decisions. Each custody decision affects the involved children for the rest of their lives.

I want to thank my coauthor, Dr. Gordon Plumb, Dr. Dianne Skafte (author and custody expert), and Dr. Richard Gardner (author and custody expert) for their contributions to my knowledge and understanding of the complexities inherent in contested custody cases.

There are individuals who are sincerely interested in improving existing laws concerning custody in order to benefit the innocent victims of contested custody (the children). I want to express my appreciation to Illinois State Senator Jim Rea, U.S. Congressman Glenn Poshard, former U.S. Congressman Ken Gray and Director Kenneth Boyle (State's Attorney Appellate Prosecutor) as some of the persons who are trying to help in humanizing child custody disputes.

My family has always been supportive of my career goals related to child custody. I sincerely appreciate their emotional support, understanding, and the patience they have demonstrated during my pursuit of professional goals related to the custody area. I, therefore, owe special thanks to my mother, Christine Turnipseed; my father, David Turnipseed; my sister, Dr. Marie Childers; my niece, Lisa Childers; my husband, Aaron Ray Lindley; and my son, David Aaron Lindley.

It would be virtually impossible for me to consider the complexities in contested custody cases without remembering the valuable "key" insights that were provided by the following individuals: Private Investigator Charlie Broy; the Hammond family (Billy Sr., Billy Jr., Billy III, Betty, and Tommy); Attorney Charles Quindry; Attorney Edwina Warner; Attorney Pam Lacey; Attorney Cheryl Powell; and Judge Terrence J. Hopkins.

Last, but not least, I want to thank all the litigants and children involved in contested custody cases who provided valuable information that contributed to an understanding of the financial and emotional implications of contested custody disputes.

I want to also acknowledge all those persons who have enough interest in custody issues to take time out of their busy schedules to read this book.

Mary E. Lindley

CONTENTS

	Page
Foreword by Glenn Poshard	v
Preface	vii

Chapter I: Introduction 3
    The Problem 3
    Extent of Problem and Limitation of Courts
      to Deal with Custody 3
    Contemporary Focus on Custody
      Evaluations and Investigations 4
    Maintaining Family Integrity and Power
      in Custody Decisions 4
    Objectives of the Book 5

**Chapter II: Ethical Principles Underlying
Structure of the Family's Team Approach** 7
    Psychological Dangers of
      Protracted Custody Litigation 7
    Importance of Ethics and Structure in
      Custody Evaluation and Investigations 8
    Ethical Principles 8
    Structure and Function of Family's Team 10
    When There is No Family's Team 11

**Chapter III: Major and Minor Criteria
for Custody** 13
    Having Clear and Relevant Guidelines for Custody 13
    The Major Criteria for Custody 13
        Psychological Parent 13
        Continuity of Relationship 16
        Emotional Stability of Parents or Guardians 16
        Continuity of Sibling Relationships 17

   Parental Flexibility... 17
   Physical Health of Parent or Guardian................... 18
  Minor Criteria for Custody....................................... 18
   Parents' Moral Character..................................... 19
   Parents' Financial, Material and Cultural Assets........... 19
   Favoring a Two Parent Home................................ 19
   Favoring the Genuine Wishes of the Child................ 19
   Favoring Child's Access to Extended Family.............. 20

Chapter IV: The Psychological Evaluation....................... 23
  Conditions and Guidelines for
   the Evaluation and Investigation........................ 23
  Evaluator's Role... 23
  Importance of Joint Parental Interview....................... 24
  Guidelines to the Parents...................................... 24
  The Various Interviews... 25
   The Joint Parental Interview................................ 26
   The Individual Interview with Parents..................... 27
   The Joint Parent-Child Interview........................... 28
   The Child Interview... 29
  Psychological Testing: Uses and Misuses..................... 30
  Putting It Together... 31

Chapter V: The Social Investigation.............................. 33
  The Role of the Investigator................................... 33
  Preparation for the Investigation.............................. 34
  Obtaining Background Information........................... 35
  Interviewing Litigants.. 35
  Interviewing Children.. 37
  Questions Used in Interviewing Children................... 39
  Interviewing Collaterals....................................... 40
  Questions Used with Collaterals.............................. 41
  Forms and Procedures... 42
  Utilizing the Forms.. 43
  The Home Visit... 44
  Assessing Major and Minor Criteria.......................... 45
  The Written Report.. 46
  Information Needed for Final Report to Court.............. 46

Contents

Meeting with the Team	47
Putting It Together Without a Team	47

Chapter VI: Taking Charge: The Team's Preparation and Meeting with the Parents 49

Differences Between the Family's Team Procedure
and Mediation/Arbitration 49
The Team's Meeting 50
The Parent and Team Meeting 50
Parental Righteousness—"The Golden Chain" 53
Verbal and Written Agreements 55

Chapter VII: Visitation 57

The Problem 57
Ideal Visitation 57
Judicial Dilemma 58
Evaluating Parents for Visitation 58
Low Quality Parenting 59
High Quality Parenting 59
High Conflict Parenting 59
Low Conflict Parenting 60
Visitation Recommendations When There
Is High Quality, Low Conflict Parenting 61
Visitation Recommendations When There Is Low Quality,
High Conflict or High Quality, High Conflict Parenting 61
General Visitation Guidelines by Age and Development 63
Special Considerations in Visitation 65
Reducing Visitation Problems 67

Chapter VIII: Special Problems in Custody Evaluations and Investigations 69

Parent-Alienation Syndrome 69
Sex and Other Abuse Charges in Custody Litigation 73

Chapter IX: Aiming for the Future 79

Ending Adversarial Litigation in Custody Disputes 79
A Pilot Project 80
Alternative Models to Adversarial Litigation 81
Concluding Comments 86

Appendices 89

1. Criteria Worksheet 90
2. Letter of Conditions and Procedures 93

3.	Parental Intake Form	95
4.	Child Care Responsibilities	97
5.	True-False Questionnaires for Litigants	99
6.	Questionnaire for Litigants	100
7.	Combination Completion/True-False Form for Litigants	101
8.	Completion Form for Litigants (1)	102
9.	Completion Form for Litigants (2)	103
10.	Completion Form for Litigants (3)	104
11.	Completion Form for Litigants (4)	105
12.	Form for Litigants	106
13.	Completion Form for Children (1)	107
14.	Completion Form for Children (2)	108
15.	Completion Form for Children (3)	109
16.	Completion Form for Children (4)	110
17.	True-False Form for Children	111
18.	Additional Questions to Utilize in Interviewing Children	112
19.	Additional Questions for Litigants in Custody Case	113
20.	Statement of Understanding Regarding Confidentiality	114
21.	Form Letter to Send to School if School Age Children	115
22.	School Report Form To Be Utilized in Custody Investigations	116
23.	Law Enforcement Form	118
24.	Collateral Form	120
25.	Verification of Employment Form	124
26.	Sample, Nonbinding, Parental Agreement	125
27.	Sample Investigative Custody Report	127
Index		129

HUMANIZING
CHILD CUSTODY DISPUTES

Chapter I

INTRODUCTION

The Problem

America has become a serially monogamous culture. Approximately 45 percent of couples who marry, divorce. Of those who divorce, most remarry. To be a child of divorce is becoming a common occurrence among the nation's youth. Due to the popularization of divorce statistics by the media, divorce is creating a cultural anxiety even in intact families. A common discussion theme among contemporary women is the topic of the latest statistics concerning the statistical "chances" of remarriage following divorce. Add to this phenomenon that wide-eyed children are more and more often asking their parents during or after a marital conflict, "Are you guys going to get divorced?" and you begin to detect the insidious effect of divorce on our culture.

Extent of Problem and Limitation of Courts to Deal With Custody

Of these divorced couples who have children, approximately 10 percent initiate child custody litigation. This statistic is on the rise. Due to several factors the wisdom of the court has risen sharply regarding litigation of these 10 percent plus. Among these factors are the pervasive legal posture that contemporary fathers and mothers have relatively equal claims to obtain custody, the overload of litigation in America upon the courts, the rising psychological sophistication of adversarial trial attorneys, and the magnitude of potential psychological evidence that can be included in any custody litigation. Paraphrasing one attorney surveyed, everything from the litigants' birth to the future may be used as evidence in custody cases. Hence, custody litigation can take as long as complicated malpractice or criminal litigation to adjudicate. Consequently, judges are recognizing their often severe limitations as domestic decision makers as well as the ascending cruelty and inefficiency of the legal adversarial process in determining custody outcomes.

More and more enlightened attorneys and judges are requesting or ordering psychological and/or homestudy investigations as an aid in decision making. While it is true that such investigations and evaluations are costly, time consuming and intrusive to the families involved, matters pertaining to the "best interests of the child" are finally entering the appropriate domain, the domain of the mental health professional. While the judicial system can legalize and legitimize relationships, it more clearly recognizes its limitations in creating, correcting, nurturing, understanding and supervising human relationships. These areas are the expertise of the mental health professional. Dr. R. Gardner[1] has painstakingly and poignantly documented the myriad of pathological consequences to litigating parties and their children of the adversarial process. It makes ultimate sense to have mental health professionals involved in a process where there is much potential for short- and long-term psychological damage.

Contemporary Focus on Custody Evaluations and Investigations

While the majority of divorcing men and women continue to make decisions regarding custody of their children, a growing number are angrily projecting their disagreements as to custody into the judicial arena for a no-holds-barred fight to the finish. It is primarily for the benefit of these unsuspecting unfortunates that the majority of this book is written. In the majority of states where the potentially destructive process of adversarial litigation is the method for resolving such disputes, we are offering a method of informed and humane investigation and evaluation geared to lessen the resultant devastation and lifelong scars of the "mine's better than yours" adversarial drama.

Maintaining Family Integrity and Power in Custody Decisions

When parents cannot or will not settle the matter of their children's well-being on their own, then it is of paramount importance that they be given the added opportunity, with the aid of appropriately trained, ethical and impartial professionals, to settle the matter of their children's welfare themselves. In so doing, they can dramatically reduce the psychological and psychophysiological damage typically resultant of adversarial litigation. Once under current law the parents have experienced the painstaking Family's Team evaluation process recommended in this book, should they continue to remain passive in deciding custody for themselves, the Family's Team approach has the advantage of providing substantial data and recommendations to the court for needed assistance in it's decision making.

Objectives of the Book

However, this book is not only for mental health, legal, and judicial professionals. This book is also for parents who wish to become more informed as to criteria and method for objective child custody and visitation recommendations. Finally, this book is foremost for legislators who, upon reading and pondering the ideas, methods, and rationale contained herein, may realize that custody matters no longer belong in adversarial court where the participants are often mis- and uninformed victims of not only their own pain and vindictiveness, but also victims of the court's unpremeditated insistence that there be winners and losers. At the conclusion of the book, we will offer more humane and efficient ideas and methods for future dispositions of custody/visitation litigation.

Chapter II

ETHICAL PRINCIPLES UNDERLYING THE STRUCTURE OF THE FAMILY'S TEAM APPROACH

Psychological Dangers of Protracted Custody Litigation

Nothing short of a threat to the physical survival of one's child can create such devastating emotional and physical stress on parents as can protracted custody litigation. One need only read Gardner's chapter on Psychiatric Disturbances of Parents and Children Caused by Custody Litigation[1] to realize the damage that can be done. Despite the best efforts of some attorneys to educate their clients to the contrary, most parents involved in litigation cling to the belief that a "win" in the courtroom means that they are okay as parents and, conversely, that a "loss" means that they are not okay. Even the usual legal standard of "best interest of the child" feeds this negative competitiveness. Once the battle lines of competition for the child or children are drawn, and with the explicit aid of their attorneys, both parents begin to assemble their arsenal of truths, half-truths, exaggerations, protestations of innocence and intimidations, and thus they prepare for battle.

It seems almost unfair for the legal system to ship these combatants and their seconds off to a mental health expert, who may be inadequately equipped to address these problems within an unfamiliar adversarial framework. Our usual clients are suffering enough emotional pain to be relatively honest and open. Not so in custody disputes. The major purpose of clients in custody disputes is to present themselves in a positive light and their adversary in a negative light. As mental health professionals, how do we arm ourselves against a parent's righteous insistence that they should be legal guardian of the children?

Importance of Ethics and Structure in Custody Evaluations and Investigations

In order to answer this, the authors had to ask themselves some questions, the most poignant being, "How is it in the best interest of children to have their parents do and say whatever is necessary to win and to malign each other publicly?" While we can understand the pressure experienced by parents and the system's adversarial collusion, it is imperative for mental health professionals to be grounded in a philosophy which minimizes damage done to all parties in such litigation. It is imperative that mental health workers involved in custody have a strong set of ethical principles from which to proceed, else risk losing themselves in the morass of righteousness, lies of omission and commission and the rigidity typical of most custody litigants.

Ethical Principles

In the majority of states where adversarial litigation remains the method by which custody is resolved, we recommend that at minimum the following ethics be strictly adhered to by forensic mental health professionals:

1. That all investigations and evaluations be performed from the standpoint of what is best for the family: namely, a Family's Team approach. This approach is congruent with the current standard of "the best interest of the child" in that what is best for the family is always in the best interest of children. If all family members are considered in recommendations for resolution of a custody dispute, this reduces the risks of continued and prolonged litigation long after initial court decisions are rendered. This principle also assists the Family's Team members in maintaining a broad, all-encompassing view of the family rather than getting caught up in the negative "either-or" competitiveness typical of adversarial litigation.
2. Natural parents and legal guardians should maintain the integrity of the family without interference from sources who have no long-term commitment and/or involvement with the family. This includes both the state as well as attorneys and mental health professionals. This principle is akin to the least intrusive method of resolving custody as advocated Goldstein et al.[2] in 1973.

As Goldstein et al.[2] have pointed out, once the litigation is over, the attorney's attention moves elsewhere and the court really does not have the capacity to supervise its own decisions. If the natural parents or guardians maintain the decision-making power over their children's lives, this greatly reduces the risk of chronic court action motivated by a disgruntled parent's sense of helplessness, despair, and vengeance. Even if parental decisions are less than optimal, that the parents make these decisions themselves enhances the likelihood of long-term compliance, often allowing the children to proceed more normally with their lives. Mental health professionals who do not recognize the wisdom of this principle and insist on having things their way "for the sake of the children" are engaging in the very same dysfunctional "either/or" relationship process which we are obliged to remedy. The old adage applies, "If you are not a part of the solution, you're a part of the problem."

3. In custody cases scheduled to be adjudicated, parents and legal guardians should always have the opportunity to obtain impartial, objective, and professional feedback and assistance as an aid in settling custody matters themselves. This is consistent with the first two principles regarding the best interest of the family and the least intrusive method. Rarely do parents possess even the rudiments of psychological knowledge needed to assess what is in the best interest of children and families concerning placement and visitation. Further, the degree of emotional involvement by parents when custody of their children is at stake is such that it is quite unlikely that they can be objective and farsighted. Consequently, those parents should have access to impartial experts as an aid in resolution.

4. Except in clearly extreme cases no child should lose access to a parent because of custody litigation. Every effort should be made to insure that children retain or even strengthen bonds to both parents. In many custody cases one of the parents is so consumed by hate and vindictiveness that they insist upon limited, supervised or even no visitation for the children with the other parent. In most cases this drastic measure is clearly to the detriment of children and ensures that the custody and visitation battle will continue, along with its pathological consequences to all parties, long after the initial court decision. This principle applies to parents who are guilty of physical and/or sexual abuse as well as parents

who are diagnosed as mentally ill or retarded. The realization of this principle is made easier by strict adherence to the first three ethical principles.

5. Mental health professionals should be clear and straightforward from the beginning with everyone involved, including the adversarial attorneys. All involved must be aware of the goals, costs, ethics and procedures to be used by the mental health professional or family's team. The parents must be aware that their disclosures are not necessarily confidential or benign, especially if the case goes to court.

Structure and Function of the Family's Team

Under current legal standards the ideal Family's Team consists of a social worker, a licensed or registered psychologist or psychiatrist and a guardian-ad-litem for the children. Each of the team members perform various tasks which when assimilated and clarified will serve as the basis for the recommendations to the family.

The Social Worker: The social worker or investigator is responsible for the following:

1. Obtaining background information on all parties involved including parents, children, and significant others (e.g., grandparents, lovers, current spouses, etc.).
2. Interviewing parents and children in respective homes.
3. Interviewing children in neutral setting such as schools, restaurants.
4. Interviewing and/or gaining information from significant others, including collateral witnesses, employers, teachers, etc.
5. Observing the behavior of parents and their children in the home environment.
6. Collecting any relevant data such as mental health data, police and/or court records, employment records, financial statements, etc.
7. Completing an assessment of Major and Minor Criteria for custody of each parent (see Chapter III).
8. Completing a final written report to the court if necessary.

The Psychologist or Psychiatrist: The psychologist or psychiatrist is responsible for the following:

1. Performing a mental status and clinical evaluation (including appro-

priate testing) of all litigants, spouses, and children who are involved in the custody dispute.
2. Interviewing parents or guardians together, separately, and individually with each of the children involved.
3. Studying data and observations provided by the investigator and integrating such material into the evaluation of the individuals and the analysis of the interactions of all parties involved.
4. Being aware of and conforming to the state custody laws and procedures.
5. Being certain that all necessary release of information forms are signed.
6. Completing an assessment of Major and Minor Criteria for custody for each litigant (see Chapter III).
7. Completing a final written report to the court if necessary.

Guardian-ad-Litem: The guardian-ad-litem is responsible for the following:

1. Protecting the legal rights of all children involved.
2. Assisting the investigator and evaluator in obtaining needed information, especially if obtaining such information requires legal intervention.
3. Providing necessary questions and challenges to the investigator and evaluator for the purpose of obtaining a thorough report which would satisfy the legal requirements of the court.
4. Participating in team meetings when conclusions and recommendations are formulated.

When There is No Family's Team

Much is lost by the use of just an evaluator or investigator whether or not a guardian-ad-litem is assigned. Nevertheless, should a single evaluator or investigator utilize the principles and procedures described in this manual, a full evaluation satisfactory to the courts can be performed.

Chapter III

MAJOR AND MINOR CRITERIA FOR CUSTODY

Having Clear and Relevant Guidelines for Custody

A decade ago there were precious few guidelines to determine what was in the best interest of children in custody determinations. A seminal work at that time was *Beyond the Best Interests of the Child*[2] which had laid the foundation for changes in Michigan custody law. Included in this critical publication were such key concepts as "psychological parent" and "continuity of relationship." While these early attempts at objectification were helpful, they were incomplete and, in some instances, inadequately defined. The critical concept of Psychological Parent, for example, was quite confusing as it often seemed that both parents or guardians were psychological parents, not just one. As a result of more research and experience over the past ten years, the following criteria were developed by the authors as instrumental in aiding families and courts in the very difficult process of custody decision making. In the not-so-distant past many court-rendered custody decisions were to a large extent competitively based on affluence, morality, influence, and judges' conscious and unconscious biases. These current criteria represent a step toward a cooperative, objective, and empathic family-centered style of decision making. Although the emotional pain of fear and anger inherent in custody disputes is not eliminated through the Family's Team approach, it is often greatly reduced. The emphasis on objectification without using the data to adversarily bludgeon the parents in a court of law is a major step toward humanizing an otherwise punitive process. The current criteria are divided into major and minor categories to reflect contemporary cultural, psychological and legal trends.

The Major Criteria for Custody

1. **Psychological Parent** — Rarely is there a case where there is only one "psychological parent" when custody is disputed. Each parent typically has his or her strengths and weaknesses and a clear-cut

preference within this criterion is the exception rather than the rule. It behooves evaluators to learn to discriminate different depths of psychological parenting and bonding rather than deciding who is and who is not a psychological parent. As Goldstein et al.[2] have pointed out, even biological ties may not be crucial in determining this critical aspect of the evaluation.

Of all the major criteria this principle of Psychological Parent is probably, at once, the most critical and the most nebulous of the evaluation. This type of bonding is more assumed through observation of certain behaviors and attitudes rather than being a "fact" submitted in evidence. Following is a list of those behaviors which indicate that an individual is a healthy psychological parent:

A. Parent acknowledges not only positive influences on family and child, but also his or her negative influences.
B. Parent allows child to express genuine feelings.
C. Parent expects some reasonable considerations from child such as age appropriate behavior and language.
D. Parent *wants* a relationship with the child and accepts responsibility for being a parent.
E. Parent does not infantalize or parentify the child.
F. Parent supports loyalty to both parents and encourages positive contact with other parent.
G. Child looks to parent for age appropriate support and guidance.
H. Child is emotionally affected by attitudes and behavior of parent. It must be remembered that even extreme anger toward a parent is indicative of psychological bonding with a parent. Often a child will openly express age-appropriate hostile feelings toward one parent, because the child knows that this parent will not collapse or reject him. On the contrary, often the child behaves carefully and adaptedly because it fears a particular parent's emotional and/or physical collapse or severe punishment. This is regarded as parentifying the child. That is where the child is unreasonably empowered to take care of the parent's feelings rather than the parent taking care of the child's feelings. Children need to test limits to grow and develop, acquiring needed empathy and a conscience.

Many of these indications of positive parent/child psychological bonding can be observed during interviews when the child meets with each parent separately as well as through questionnaires. Children are not usually so sophisticated as adults and consequently are more obvious in exposing their attitudes and behaviors reflective of differential psychological bonding. Such questions as, "If I were in the hospital and only one parent could stay in the room with me, I would want _____ to be with me" are often quite revealing. An exception to this is the "brainwashed" child or a child suffering from Parent Alienation Syndrome (discussed in Chapter VIII). Some uncoached children whose innocence is left intact in spite of the tension created by adversarial parents, often come right out and say, "I would like to live with my mom (or dad) and visit with my dad (or mom)."

Usually the most important variable in determining the parent with whom the child has the deepest psychological bond is recognizing which parent has had the most time and responsibility for the child during its formative years. Formative years is here defined as approximately from birth to age 12. In most cases this is the mother.

In summary, a child's needs go beyond the obvious bodily necessities. Paraphrasing Goldstein et al.,[2] a psychological parent need not be a biological parent or even a blood relative. If a child is uprooted from the major psychological parent, regressive tendencies soon become evident. Inferior school performance, social withdrawal, hypersensitivity, aggression, clinging, physical symptoms, and indecisiveness are all common symptoms of the uprooted and insecure child. Depending on the child's age, he or she is confronted with various developmental tasks and crises. When a child is interrupted in these tasks to the point of insecurity, he or she invariably regresses to an earlier stage of development. For example, a child who was learning how to interact and share with peers may, under the fear of losing a trusted and reliable psychological parent, revert back to basic trust issues, becoming clingy and constantly testing his or her primary relationship. Typical regressive behaviors of insecure children include food refusals, gastrointestinal problems, sleep disorder, bedwetting, and excessive crying. The types of regressive behaviors indicated can usually be ascertained by careful questioning of the parents and children about the children's reaction as they are spending time at each parent's home. Of all the criteria listed, this is the most central and crucial. Many of the other criteria listed are but footnotes to and evidence of this critical psychological relationship.

2. **Continuity of Relationship:** This criteria of placement is amply described by Goldstein et al.[2] In summary, this principle states that a child needs the stability of an uninterrupted relationship. All children's mental processes are relatively unstable during their formative years. "Smooth growth is arrested or disrupted when upheavals and changes in the external world are added to the internal ones."[2] This principle regarding the placement of children is important until adolescence. Should any change of custody be requested when the children have resided with a specific parent or guardian for a prolonged period of time, there should be clear, factual evidence of repeated dangers to the child's physical or emotional well-being prior to any change. Generally, this criterion carries substantial weight when children are under six years and becomes increasingly less critical until the child reaches adolescence. The continuity factor reflects the general truism that external disruptions earlier in life are more likely to cause psychological harm to development than later disruptions. The specific length of time a child is residing with one parent when it would be imprudent to change custody varies with age. Generally the younger the child (under 12 years) the more developmentally damaging such a custody change could be and the briefer the time period required to satisfy the continuity criterion.

3. **Emotional Stability of Parents or Guardians:** This criterion for placement is evaluated by interview behavior (including behavior in the waiting room) and the interaction of the two principals while together with the examiner. Also, the homestudy and interviewing of significant collaterals can reveal much data as to emotional stability of the litigants. Past records concerning mental health or legal difficulties are also useful. Especially revealing is the manner in which the principals understand the concepts of "brainwashing" and "loyalty conflict" as it relates to their children. Supplemental to the behavioral data which is assessed, a Minnesota Multiphasic Personality Inventory (MMPI) should be administered. Often this inventory will support clinical judgments. Special care should be taken in interpreting the validity scales as the very nature of the evaluation and the adversarial process forces most people into

presenting themselves as better than they really are. As Gardner[1] has pointed out, care should be taken in administering psychological labels in potential adversarial litigation. He justifiably maintains that a clear description of behavior is superior to a diagnostic label should the case end up in court. One of the more useful signs of emotional maturity is the attitudes of the contesting parties toward each other. A very negatively aggressive attitude toward the other, however justified, is not a sign of adult maturity characteristic of emotional stability and sound psychological parenting. Care should be given to assessing this characteristic as the very process of adversarial litigation with its insistence of having "good guys" and "bad guys" fosters these aggressive tendencies in even the most stable of individuals.

4. **Continuity of Sibling Relationships:** When there are two or more children involved in a custody dispute, it is generally in the best interest of the family for the children not to be separated. Most separations seem to occur because the court attempts to appease a parent by dividing the children equally as though they were marital property. The only time we have recommended the splitting of siblings is when the siblings had already been living with the other parent for several years.

5. **Parental Flexibility:** Custody placements should take into account not only the overall flexibility of the conflicted parties, but more specifically, the flexibility of each toward contact and visitation with the other parent or guardian and their extended family. Following a final determination, children should not be subject to continued brainwashing and loyalty conflicts. For most children under age 14 years, it is impossible to have a separate, different, and healthy relationship with both parents when the adults are continually hostile and conflictual with each other. Children must be free to relate to all members of the family and extended family in order to overcome the trauma of divorce and custody conflicts and regain some consistency and stability. Parental flexibility can be determined in individual and joint interviews as well as assessing responses to questionnaires. If the parents have been separated or divorced for some time prior to the Family Team's evaluation, the visitation data for the period usually reveals parental attitudes and behavior concerning flexibility. Were the children allowed free access to the other parent including telephone calls? Is there chronic

lateness in returning children? Are there constant complaints that the children are always in emotional turmoil when they are returned or brought to the other parent's home? This is an especially important criterion, not only for custody determination, but also for visitation recommendations (see Chapter VII).

6. **Physical Health of Parent or Guardian:** Should a contesting party's physical health be sufficiently impaired so as to negate a relatively stable and unbroken relationship with the child or children, this should be considered strongly. Such cases where the death of a parent is expected within a short time or where the parent needs to constantly go away for longer periods of treatment must be considered. Severe physical handicaps need to be carefully and objectively evaluated in order to make the best possible recommendations for the child's development.

Minor Criteria for Custody

1. **Parents' Moral Character:** Contemporary moral standards are much different than in previous generations. Today's standards reflect a mixed blessing of permissiveness and human acceptance. Consequently it is recommended that this criterion be used with caution and self-awareness of one's own bias. In typical custody disputes the conflicting parties are quick to exaggerate the other's moral imperfections and even to invent some. Care must be taken to utilize only those moral characteristics which are acknowledged or documented. Accusations of physical and sexual abuse are on the increase in custody disputes and, in the absence of proof, should be considered as red flags of possible manipulation. Physical and sexual abuse allegations will be dealt with in more depth in another chapter.

Current legal standards require that an individual's lifestyle must be proven to be detrimental to a child before it can be used as a criterion to dispute custody. Consequently, it is not any longer legally relevant whether one parent is homosexual or bisexual unless it can be shown conclusively how this sexual preference has specifically affected the child or children in question in a negative way. Psychological research predominantly supports this legal standard. Examples of questionable morality regarding child custody are professional or chronic felons, proven spouse abuse, and documented child physical or sex abuse. Parental infidelity is not ordinarily considered in this category unless there has been a pattern of infidelity which has definitely affected the child or children in a negative way. Performing sex in the presence of children or leaving small children unattended for long periods of time while engaged in sexual behavior are examples of such questionable morality. Religion or lack thereof are not criteria which are to be routinely utilized in this category.

2. **Parents' Financial, Material and Cultural Assets:** This criteria is potentially a volatile issue when dealing with the emotionally laden issue of child custody. Nevertheless, it is an issue of some import in custody decisions and should not be avoided simply because it is a distasteful subject. This criteria should never be used to countermand major criteria regardless of the difference in material assets between the parties.

3. **Favoring a Two Parent Home:** Research indicates that it is generally better for children to have two parents in the home. Hodges[3] has an excellent chapter on the problems inherent in single parent homes. A synopsis of his views include:

   A. The culture is organized for two parent homes.
   B. Single parenting limits the wisdom of the family.
   C. Emotional support may be more limited.
   D. Sex role development may be impaired.
   E. Often children experience abandonment issues which affect their sense of self-esteem.
   F. There is no compensation for single parent overprotectiveness or underprotectiveness.
   G. Child care is a constant problem.

When the mother is the single parent, finances are apt to suffer. Women earn about 65 percent of the amount earned by men. Approximately 92 percent of all single parents are mothers.

For a thorough understanding of the framework and necessity for this criterion read Chapter 8 of Hodges' book, *Interventions for Children of Divorce*.[3]

4. **Favoring the Genuine Wishes of the Child:** Many parents are perplexed that the wishes of a child are not considered more critical to the outcome of a custody evaluation. In our system of evaluation the wishes of children under 13 years are considered a minor criterion. There are two major reasons for this. First of all, children

often do not possess the objectivity or experience to be able to reasonably evaluate what is in their best interest. Often their reasons for preferring to live with one parent over the other are quite superficial, reflecting immediate gratification. We have heard such reasons as "Dad is nicer," "We go more places," or even "Dad can buy me more things." Most recently, one five year old stated that he preferred to live with his mom, "unless dad gets me a dog." In most evaluations the children already live with one parent and visit the other. It is not uncommon for children to prefer the parent whom they visit because they receive special treatment when visiting as that parent does not have the daily responsibility for them. It is our contention that most children under 13 or 14 cannot and should not make such complex and abstract decisions.

Secondly, while we contend that children under 13 or 14 cannot make such decisions, neither should they have the power or responsibility to decide where they will live. That is too much pressure for most children and often places them in an untenable loyalty conflict. The amount of brainwashing and solicitation of children's affections which is routine in most custody disputes would skyrocket, placing the child in serious psychological jeopardy.

There are many methods which can be used to determine a child's preference without direct questioning. These methods will be discussed in Chapters IV and V. For adolescents age 13 and beyond this criterion assumes major importance if the adolescent has a preference and his reasons are not based on a Parent-Alienation Syndrome (see Chapter VIII) or other serious pathology.

5. **Favoring Child's Access to Extended Family:** Many children enjoy the advantages of frequent contact with extended family while their parents are married and live together. Often one or both parents have extended family in the geographic area where the once intact family lived. Relationships with extended family provide children with a rich diversity of experience as well as a sense of belonging and security. This criterion is meant to safeguard these relationships not only from a custodial parent moving out of the geographic area, but also from vindictive and inflexible parents who would refuse or make such contact difficult for their ex-spouse's extended family. This criterion should be used in conjunction with the Major Criterion of Favoring the More Flexible Parent.

As these criteria provide the basis for the custody recommendations to the parents and potentially to the court, it is critical to be clear and concise regarding results and the data supporting the results. For this reason a special criteria worksheet is used by the Team during the final stages of the evaluation (see Appendix 1). This sheet is used as the basis for the meeting with the parents and, if necessary, as the groundwork for a formal, written court report.

Chapter IV

THE PSYCHOLOGICAL EVALUATION

Conditions and Guidelines for the Evaluation and Investigation

Prior to the actual interview with the potential litigants, children and important collaterals, the evaluator should supply all parties and their attorneys with a statement of conditions and procedures for undertaking the evaluation. As a private practitioner I do not undertake a custody evaluation unless I am agreed upon as evaluator by all parties and their attorneys or a judge has ordered all parties to cooperate in an evaluation. Ideally, a court order should be required as this safeguards against disgruntled parties terminating the evaluation prematurely. To this end the statement of conditions (including fees) and usual procedures (see appendix 2) is sent to all parties and attorneys. This form is sent regardless of whether the evaluation is court ordered or agreed upon by all parties. The use of adversarial experts or evaluators should be avoided in nearly all cases. Contradictory testimonies cancel each other out and tend to alienate the judiciary, attorneys, and the public concerning psychologists and psychiatrists. The Hinckley and Patty Hearst trials with their parade of expensive experts all contradicting each other has had a justifiably negative impact on psychological credibility in the courtroom.

Evaluators Role

When there is a Team involved, the evaluator and investigator should coordinate responsibilities to avoid unnecessary and costly duplication. In the letter which accompanies the evaluator's conditions, fees and procedures, appointment dates should be offered. It is imperative that all parties and all children show up for the initial interview at the same time. I inform all parties that we will spend about three to four hours for the initial evaluation. I have encountered some resistance to this procedure, as quite often one parent will state that it would be too traumatic for them or the children to see the ex-spouse. I simply explain the general reasons for the joint interview and have only once encountered a refusal by any party to attend the initial evaluation jointly. My explanation to parties and their attorneys, if needed, is simply that I learn invaluable information about all parties by their joint attendance at the initial interview. The one exception to this success is one mother who refused to bring her child to an interview with the natural father because the child had not been told that this was her father and the mother steadfastly refused to do so.

Importance of Joint-Parental Interview

It is extremely difficult to get reliable, objective, and factual data from parents in a custody dispute. The requirement that both parties interview with the evaluator together affords the opportunity to confront and clarify the situation personally, often giving the evaluator important cues as to who is telling the truth. Also, this procedure affords the evaluator the opportunity to view children's behavior in the presence of both parents. Waiting room behavior by the parents and children can reveal the presence and degree of loyalty conflicts as well as crucial clues as to who is the more psychological parent. Regardless of the legal justification for mental health evaluations in custody matters, evaluation and investigative personnel need to remember that we are essentially *intruding* into the most sensitive and private aspects of people's lives. This task should be undertaken only with sensitive respect toward the parents and the children. Too often mental health professionals forget their roles and duties as helpers and objective analysts and act more like attorneys and police.

Guidelines to the Parents

In the initial joint interview with both parents it is imperative that the evaluator is clear and thorough in his or her explanations and descriptions. I inform the litigants jointly of the following:

1. That nothing that is said by anyone is necessarily confidential.
2. That I will attempt during and following the evaluation/investigation to assist them to reach an out-of-court settlement of custody and visitation.

3. That I stand for the integrity of the family unit and will not judge any one individual as "good" or "bad."
4. That honesty is imperative. That I cannot be of service to the parents or their children if I am told lies of omission or commission. That any lies encountered in the evaluation or investigation will reflect upon their character and will be taken into account in my conclusions and recommendations should the case go to court.
5. That I understand that the adversarial process itself will tend to make each blame and accuse the other of things both true and false and that I look upon such blaming as reflective of questionable emotional maturity (a major criteria). Further, that such blaming and insults of either of the children's parents is never in the best interests of the children, especially when done in front of the children.
6. That in the event of either parent deciding to go to court that the judge will in all likelihood take my or the Team's recommendations quite seriously.
7. That money spent on attorneys, psychologists, and court costs could be better utilized by providing for the children's material needs.

In going over at least these seven points during the initial interview I have found that parents have generally been more truthful and cooperative with me and with each other than when I did not utilize this procedure. I have found that this time spent at the very beginning of the process sets the tone for an eventual cooperative resolution to custody by the parents. Prior to my use of the process outlined in this chapter, I went to court on nearly all custody cases. During the past four years I have had to testify in court only twice.

The Various Interviews

Following the lead of Gardner,[1] I conduct several types of joint interviews depending upon the age and number of children:

1. The joint parental interview;
2. The individual parent interview;
3. The joint parent-child interview with each parent separately;
4. The individual child interview (for children over five years);

5. The joint parent-child interview with both parents and a child (for adolescents especially).

Often parents who could lie or exaggerate in the joint parent interview cannot bring themselves to lie in front of their children who know the truth. I cannot emphasize enough the tremendous advantage of this process in obtaining truth over the courtroom procedure where parents are represented through their attorneys. Naturally the evaluator reserves the right to request an interview with any combination of the principals involved. Often, especially with children in puberty or beyond, I conduct an interview with both parents and all the children together.

The Joint Parental Interview

During the initial joint session with the parents the following details should be taken care of:

1. Any release of information needed should be signed. These include releases for teachers and school personnel, medical doctors, past psychologists or psychiatrists, inpatient or outpatient treatment, court or prison records, military records, work records.
2. A listing of any collateral witnesses whom the litigants regard as able to provide crucial information.
3. A groundwork laid for an out-of-court settlement as outlined earlier in this chapter (e.g., Guidelines To the Parents).

Once the more structured portion of the joint interview is accomplished, the more open-ended portion of the joint interview may begin. I often start this by asking each of the parents to state what happened in the marriage. The responses to this open-ended question usually provide me with key clues as to personality and the extent of unresolved conflict that is left over from the marital breakup. I look for blaming, guilt trips, suffering, passivity, ability to empathize and understand, flexibility, and other characteristics which reflect upon the parents' abilities as psychological parents and their emotional maturity. Also, this is an excellent opportunity to assess the continuity of relationship with the children and who has been the primary caretaker. When parents are interviewed separately each often overstates the quantity and quality of his/her own child care and there is practically no discernable method to realistically rate these critical dimensions. When interviewed together the evaluator can get a much clearer picture of these important criteria. It is only in joint interviews that allegations can be directly refuted by the parties themselves without the aid of a spokesperson (the attorney). Gardner[1] has pointed out the tremendous advantage that the evaluator has over the court in getting at the truth concerning typical custody allegations. The evaluator and investigator are the only ones who have the opportunity to experience an interplay among the parents and children. The court must rely on information being filtered through the attorneys in court. Parents never have the opportunity to retort or confront in the courtroom as they risk contempt of court.

In many instances each parental allegation is refuted by the other parent leaving the examiner with little of substance. Even if the examiner believes one party, should this allegation be made an issue in court an opposing attorney can greatly jeopardize the evaluator's argument when the alleged guilty party has refuted the allegation. Simply believing someone without some substantial proof is not well accepted in courts. For this reason the joint interview, with its more immediate prospects of agreements or even admissions to allegations by one or both parties, is an invaluable tool for the examiner. Actual admissions and direct statements by the parties are much more acceptable should the case go to court than any battery of psychological tests, diagnostic labels or therapeutic "hunches."

The Individual Interview with Parents

During the individual interview with parents the evaluator should review with the individual parent any unusual statements or opinions made on the parental questionnaires (see Appendices 3–12). Examples of something unusual would be that it was established in the interview that Mr. X had been to prison ten years earlier; however, this was not listed in the appropriate place on the questionnaire. With the aid of the parental questionnaire there is much that the evaluator can use to trigger responses from the parents reflective of their emotional maturity and capability as psychological parents.

Also during the individual interview it is important to offer each parent the opportunity to tell you anything they believe relevant to the child's best interest or about their reasons for believing they are the better choice as permanent custodian of the children. When a parent presents him or herself in a manner indicative of severe psychopathology a formal mental status interview should be administered in addition to the usual MMPI. A list of evaluator/investigator questions for parents is listed in Appendix 19.

The Joint Parent-Child Interview:

This is a strategic interview with regard to gathering firsthand data on how the children react to each parent when in the same room. How does the child respond to that parent when under stress? Is that parent responsive to the child's needs? Does that parent treat the child's needs with respect or with indifference or even hostility? Often this is a very awkward and difficult interview for the parents as well as the children. The evaluator does well to have some icebreaking comments or questions which can reduce the tension. Depending upon the age of the children (usually above 6 or 7), I offer to the children, "How long has it been since you've had a chance to have a good talk with your dad (or mom)?" or to the parent, "Why don't you tell your son/daughter how you feel being here today?" I continue to ask relatively benign questions until the communication begins to flow more smoothly. I often "sneak in" a little therapy at times by either asking the children if they realize they're not going to lose a parent over the marital breakup, or by asking the parents if they have reassured the children that they both will be there for them regardless of who gets custody. Often quite revealing personality characteristics come to light at this time. Some parents have been so blatant as to state in front of the children that they won't get to see the children much if they don't have custody because the other parent will make it difficult. I have even had one father tell his teenage son who had chosen to live with his mother that he would not even see him unless the boy changed his mind and lived with him. The boy changed his mind. In any event, this portion of the interview is an opportunity to check for parental manipulations, reflections of emotional stability, and ability to be a healthy psychological parent.

If there are parental allegations of abuse or neglect these can be brought up in this interview to check for accuracy and/or to see if there is resolution between the parent and child about past parental mistakes. For example:

Evaluator: There is some talk of your having bruised Jimmy a couple of times in the past, Mr. Jones. Do you remember this, Jimmy?
Jimmy (8 years old): Ah, yes, I think so.
Evaluator (nonpunitively): Have you two talked this over, Mr. Jones?
Mr. Jones (defensively): He knows I didn't mean it.

This dialogue would reveal poor psychological parenting and negatively reflect upon the father's emotional maturity as the father's statement was clearly avoidant and indicated a need to protect his own feelings at the expense of his son's feelings.

The Child Interview

There is generally not much to be gained by individual interviews with preverbal or children under 5 or 6 years of age. Their reasoning is usually quite simplistic and irrelevant to custody. Children of this age are quite immediate and have little capacity to deal with the ramifications of their otherwise age appropriate, immature whims. With children under 5 or 6 little credibility should be given to their preferences, but particular attention should be given to the interaction with each of the parents separately and together as well as to their waiting room behavior. With such children the evaluator should pay heed to expressions of affection, seating preferences and spontaneous gestures. It is important to remember that parents are usually on their best behavior when in the evaluation process and the evaluator must attempt to separate playacting a good parent from spontaneously being a good parent.

With children judged mature enough by the examiner (usually over 5 or 6 years) it is important to first gain rapport by introducing non-threatening subjects. Talking about sports, school activities, friends, goals, etc. can provide a basis of trust and warmth between the evaluator and child. The child should have filled out various child questionnaires (see Appendices 13–17) and this can serve as a stimulus to questions reflective of the custody criteria. For example:

Evaluator: I noticed that the person you admire most is your mother. That sounds wonderful. Can you tell me more about why?

or

Evaluator: I noticed that the one thing you would change about your mom would be her drinking. How do you feel about her drinking?.... How does she act when she drinks?", etc.

Otherwise, the list of children's questions listed in Chapter V (and in Appendix 18) provide ample material with which to gather important information from children reflective of the Major and Minor Criteria.

Generally, the closer a child is to adolesence the more weight his or her preferences should carry, especially when the child is relatively normal developmentally and is not suffering from Parent Alienation Syndrome (see Chapter VIII).

Psychological Testing: Uses and Misuses

Unless there is a clear reason for doing so, a full battery of psychological testing is unnecessary. I prefer the administration of the Minnesota Multiphasic Personality Inventory (MMPI) to the parents and the stepparents. The MMPI with its emphasis upon validity as well as its well researched clinical and research scales provides an objective comparison for our clinical judgment. Of particular interest to the evaluator are the validity scales where attempts to "look good" often stand out and can help confirm clinical impressions. Only when there is extremely clear clinical evidence in addition to the MMPI results should a formal diagnosis of any of the parents be assigned. Of much more credibility to parents and courts are descriptions of actual behavior which reflect on their capacity to parent. It is much clearer and far more potent to give a description of how a parent is chronically late, has sometimes not even shown up for visitation (with appropriate excuses, of course), and is two months behind on child support than it is to state that this parent has a passive-aggressive personality. Should cases go to court any reasonable attorney can have a grand time making evaluators operationally define terms and support very ambiguous and abstract diagnostic categories. Diagnoses often bring the credibility of the evaluator into question. When this happens the focus of the court hearing is shifted from what is relevant to the best interest of the child and family to whether or not the evaluator is credible. If the MMPI is used, it should be interpreted by a legally and professionally competent evaluator. In most states this must be done by a licensed psychologist or psychiatrist.

Other forms of testing utilized by the authors are the various questionnaires and sentence-completion tests found in the appendices. Care should be given to the procedure for test taking. Children should fill out or otherwise provide answers to these questionnaires away from their parents, at the evaluator's office or with the investigator. Having the secretary administer these questionnaires is appropriate. This evaluator was justifiably confronted by an astute attorney in court because a child had not only filled out the questionnaire with only the mother present in the waiting room, but upon closer scrutiny of the questionnaire, it was evident that the mother had actually done much of the writing.

In cases where it appears that any child may be suffering from some serious psychopathological or psychophysiological disorder, a full clinical evaluation should be made including appropriate diagnosis, prognosis and recommendations. It is often helpfully revealing how parents handle the afflictions of their children. Do they blame the other parent? Do they dismiss clear indication of pathology? Do they become hysterical? Do they reinforce the pathology?

In summary, testing can be an appropriate and useful tool if used sparingly and with sound clinical justification. Diagnostic labeling should be avoided for adults in most cases but can be essential for more seriously disturbed children.

Putting It Together

Following all interviews, testing, review of clinical notes and forms, collateral evidence and reports, the examiner utilizes the Criteria Worksheet (see Appendix 1) to assess each parent's strengths and weaknesses as they relate to the Major and Minor Criteria. This should be done separately from the investigator when there is Team involvement. A more detailed explanation and examples of the process following evaluation can be found in Chapter VI.

Chapter V

THE SOCIAL INVESTIGATION

The Role of the Investigator

The functions of the Team's investigator in child custody litigation is an invaluable aid to the Team's analysis and to the conclusions they draw. The investigator has access to "in vivo" data concerning the litigants and their children. The investigator is not limited by the artificial atmosphere of the evaluator's consulting room. The investigator has the luxury of showing up unannounced at the litigant's homes or visiting with the children in such neutral settings as ice cream parlors, restaurants, or school. For example, the authors once worked as a team in a case involving temporary custody filed by grandparents due to alcoholism and spouse abuse by the parents. During this investigation, the investigator kept attempting to visit the parents in the morning at their home. Each attempt to visit was met with no response even though the investigator was certain that the mother was at home. Finally, the investigator was able to gain entrance only to be told by the father that his wife was too sick to even see the investigator. When the investigator insisted upon just having a minute with the mother it was discovered that the father had beaten her physically and she was too afraid of him to expose the spouse abuse. While these same individuals were in the evaluator's office they presented themselves as loving, caring parents and that the husband had long ago stopped the physical abuse of his wife, especially in front of the children. Without the investigator's tireless efforts this critical data would not have surfaced and the results and recommendations would have been quite different.

In general the investigator has the responsibility to complete a thorough and objective analysis of the following:

1. An investigation into the parenting abilities of each parent (focusing especially on strengths and weaknesses).
2. An investigation into the needs and feelings of any children involved.
3. An investigation of each parent's allegations concerning the other

(especially those allegations which have a direct effect on the children).
4. An investigation into each parent's past parenting abilities, current parenting abilities, and potential for assuming future parenting responsibilities.
5. An investigation of each litigant as it relates to the Major and Minor Criteria from Chapter III.
6. An investigation of each litigant's income, source of income, and work history.
7. An investigation of any significant collateral contacts, especially including extended family with whom the children have contact, and the children's schools.
8. An investigation of the home of each litigant as to appropriateness and necessities for children.

On many occasions significant information would have been lost without a thorough investigation. For example, due to a thorough investigation we have discovered children secretly living with grandparents rather than parents, welfare fraud, lying about income, and many other bits of false information that were presented to the evaluator in the office.

Preparation for the Investigation

In preparation it is essential to review the court order that provides the mandate for the investigator to be involved. Under current law the investigator is usually a specialist within the state child welfare agency and needs to be court appointed. It is critical to clearly understand who the litigants are, names and ages of children involved, and any current court decisions affecting the parents and children such as temporary custody and visitation schedules. It behooves the investigator to contact each adversarial attorney to obtain their lists of allegations which need scrutiny. This practice saves time and helps prevent the escalation of allegations during the evaluative and investigative process. An important procedural rule is to *never* just talk with one attorney as that can lead to investigative bias. Conference calls with both attorneys at once is a tool which can enhance objectivity and professionalism with the adversarial attorneys. Should a guardian-ad-litem (GAL) be appointed, the investigator should contact the GAL and obtain a list of his or her needs.

Some forms and questionnaires should be sent to each litigant so that this information can be obtained prior to the actual investigation (see Appendices 3 and 12). Also, any court dates should be known to the investigator as well as the entire Team so that realistic planning and timely results are available without constantly changing court dates at the last minute. Court appearances and cancellations cause a great deal of anxiety and resentment and often add avoidable tension between the parties and affect the children negatively.

As can be noted, there is no mention of contact with the presiding judge prior to actual trial. It is not recommended that any Team member initiate contact with the judge prior to a court appearance. Should the judge contact the investigator, it is recommended that any Team member answer questions if possible in an objective manner. Should the case go to court, the investigator and other Team members need to retain their positions of objectivity and not be attempting to influence a judge without all parties being present.

Obtaining Background Information

An integral part of preparation is obtaining relevant background information. Much of the background needed can be obtained from the Parental Intake Form sent out to parents (see Appendix 3). The important areas in a social history include: educational background, marital history, employment history, income and source of income, current living conditions, health, religion, activities, history of drugs or alcohol abuse or legal difficulties (regardless of disposition), self-assessment of parental strengths and weaknesses, child care plans, and a list of references as to character and parenting practices. If any of the litigants have remarried or are living with or will live with or remarry following the custody outcome, it is essential to gather information about these individuals as well. This basis will provide the investigator with specific direction during actual interviews without having to use a time consuming "shot-gun" approach to questioning. When the investigator has all of the above preparatory tasks completed he or she is ready for the actual investigative work.

Interviewing Litigants

After obtaining the initial background information of each parent, the next step in the investigative process is to begin interviewing each parent on two or three separate occasions. During the first interview, it is important to obtain a clear understanding of the main reasons for the pending contested custody litigation, the legal status of the case, the length of time the parents have been separated or divorced, the major problems in the marriages, and an understanding of where the children have resided since the marital conflicts began to the present time. If any information is not clear in the questionnaire completed by the litigant, an interview can help to clarify the litigant's responses to the questions.

A second interview can provide an opportunity to ask questions designed to help assess parenting abilities. Please refer to Appendix 19 for a listing of some of the interview questions we have found to be beneficial in obtaining information that would relate to parenting abilities and/or beliefs.

The second interview can also provide an opportunity for the investigator to ask the parent to complete forms designed to help assess major criteria utilized in the assessment phase. It is helpful to have the forms completed in the presence of the investigator to prevent an opportunity for the parent to discuss the questions with anyone else. If a parent is illiterate or does not read well, the interviewer or a substitute can read the questions and write down the litigant's responses to each question. The parent should sign his name and date to each form completed.

The third interview is basically an interview in which any allegations or concerns about each parent can be discussed with that parent so the interviewer can obtain both sides of each main area of concern.

It is beneficial for the custody investigator to conduct at least one joint interview with both parents present as well as to observe both parents with the child or children during a scheduled observation. Being able to observe facial expressions of parents, gestures, and other visual cues while they are together can provide relevant information in trying to determine the truth of some of the allegations. At times a parent will tell one version of a story and then give contrasting information in the presence of the spouse or ex-spouse. In this particular interview allegations or expressed concerns can be discussed with both parents present. The verbal exchange during this type of interview is usually invaluable in helping to assess the veracity of information given by each parent, and can also help create a clearer picture of the extent to which each parent meets or does not meet the Major and Minor Criteria. Valuable insights can usually be obtained by utilizing at least one joint interview of parents that could not be obtained any other way.

It is also extremely beneficial to observe the litigants together with the child or children in a scheduled one-hour observation in a neutral setting such as a park or restaurant. In our experience, a child will usually relate in a more positive way to the litigant with whom the child is more emotionally bonded. There is usually consistency in information obtained in terms of observation, answers in interview questions, and answers in completed forms that all help in determining the Major and Minor Criteria. It is also our experience that the parent who has been the most active participant in assuming responsibilities for child care tasks and for being involved in recreational and/or educational activities with a child will be the litigant who exhibits more of this same caring type of behavior during the visits.

Interviewing Children

In interviewing children (ages 5 years old or older), it is important to utilize a neutral setting as the place for the interview such as the school or the park (in warm weather). This investigator has also found it beneficial to interview children in relaxed settings such as taking a child to a favorite restaurant in order to talk. An office is usually one of the least relaxed settings for a child, and if one of the litigant's homes is utilized for the interview, it is possible that a child might not feel as comfortable in relating relevant information (especially negative) about that parent. It is essential that each child be interviewed privately and separately and that neither parent be present for any of the interviews with the children.

It is important before beginning an interview with a child to assess the child's understanding of what it means to tell the truth, to try to help the child understand the purpose of the interview, and to try to help the child to feel as relaxed as possible. It is important to stress to the child that the main request is that the information be answered truthfully and that the child's ideas, beliefs, and feelings are the focus of the interviews.

Utilizing questions such as what a child likes best and least about each parent helps to gain an insight into the way the child perceives each parent. Since each parent in all probability will present two totally diverse views of most areas covered, the interview with each child helps to try to determine which parent has been the most active participant in assuming responsibilities for child-care tasks, which parent spends more time in providing recreational and/or educational activities or opportunities for the child, and which parent is emotionally closest to the child.

Having children complete forms designed by the authors can further aid in understanding the child's perceptions of each parent. It is essential that children complete forms while in a neutral setting. Also, dependent upon the child's age, he or she needs to understand that although you will respect their confidence, the information obtained from the child is important and may be talked over with others. With late puberty or adolescent children, I inform them more clearly that what they say may be shared with others and will be taken seriously in my conclusions.

An important consideration is always a child's perception of each parent, whether it is based on fact, fantasy, or a combination of the two. It is particularly important to find out a teenager's ideas, preference for living arrangements, etc., as judges appropriately tend to give more weight to the wishes of a teenager. If a teenager resists living with a mother, and the reasons are based on understandable logical thinking, then it would be difficult to try to legally force the teenager to live with the mother since teenagers can be extremely disruptive. Even the court cannot effectively force compliance of teenagers as they do not have the resources to monitor their decisions effectively.

Parents are quite capable of trying to sabotage a child's time with the other parent. Common maneuvers include saying a child can't be at the other parent's home for a scheduled visit due to illness, not having transportation, or the child having an important extracurricular activity. Other techniques for sabotaging visits include being two or three hours late in getting the child to the scheduled meeting place, encouraging the child to create a scene saying that he or she does not want to visit the parent, or threatening that if the other parent doesn't pay court-ordered child support, the child will not be allowed a scheduled visit with the parent (even if the child wants to). In one particularly extreme case, the mother and stepfather of a child arranged to give visitation to the father at a public location. Secretly, they had arranged with a television station to be present with a videotape camera to record the child who was going to dramatically reject the father on tape for the local news.

"Brainwashing" is often readily utilized to try to poison a child's mind about the other parent. The younger the child and the earlier the brainwashing begins, the easier it is to turn the child against the other parent. Calls alleging suspected child abuse or neglect of a child by one of the parents (without any factual basis) can be utilized to try to deny access to the child by one of the parents. This can be accomplished successfully if a parent utilizes professionals who will help the parent prevent the alleged perpetrator of abuse to have custody of or visits with the child pending an investigation of the allegation. Unfortunately, there are many such professionals, especially in state-run or supported legal and child care agencies. A parent who wants to prevent a child from seeing the other parent has at his or her disposal a variety of sophisticated methods to try to accomplish this goal. This is one reason contested custody cases are usually quite complex and difficult to assess.

To help counter the myriad of maneuvers and allegations of one parent attempting to sabotage the relationship of the other parent with the children, it is essential to utilize the interviews with the children in such a manner as to ascertain the likelihood of such parental allegations. Unsuspecting children will usually be truthful if addressed directly or even indirectly about their parents' typical subversive techniques. This truthfulness is, of course, compromised when the child is "brainwashed" or suffers from a Parent Alienation Syndrome (see Chapter VIII). Nevertheless, the child interviews in a neutral setting can shed considerable light on the veracity of parental allegations and sabotage maneuvers.

Questions Used in Interviewing Children

First, assess the child's ability or understanding of telling the truth. Once you have established that the child knows what telling the truth means, then the following questions may be utilized:

1. What is your name?
2. How old are you? What kinds of activities do you enjoy?
3. What grade of school are you in (if school age)?
4. What is your understanding of why I want to talk to you?
5. Can you describe your mother, your stepfather, if appropriate?
6. Describe your father for me, your stepmother, if appropriate.
7. What do you like best about being in your mother's home?
8. Is there anything about being in your mother's home that makes you unhappy?
9. What do you like best about being in your father's home?
10. Is there anything about being in your father's home that makes you unhappy?
11. Do you ever get into trouble at your mother's or father's home?

12. If so, what do you get in trouble for in each home? What method of discipline is used by each parent?
13. Describe a typical day at your mother's house.
14. Describe a typical day at your father's house.
15. What kinds of activities do you and your mom do together? What kinds of activities do you and your dad do together? Do you have any idea who spends more time with you, your mom or your dad?
16. If you had three wishes, what would you wish for?
17. Do you have a preference regarding who you would rather live with? If so, what is it and what are the reasons for your preference?
18. If you had a problem you needed to discuss, who would you want to talk to and why?

Additional questions for children may be found in Appendix 18.

Interviewing Collaterals

Interviewing collaterals is a valuable source of information, particularly in terms of assessing the extent of truth, if any, to allegations listed in petitions. It is especially enlightening not to pursue interviews with just the collaterals a person lists as a reference, but also to interview collaterals not listed by litigants if the collateral would be a potential source of relevant information.

Consider the example of a parent who filed for custody of a child and obtained temporary legal custody of the child. An allegation was made that the child was not actually living in that particular parent's home but in a relative's home (a relative who had no legal involvement and was not a party to the custody proceeding). In person contacts with neighbors can confirm the truth or falsehood of such an allegation. If several neighbors have never observed a child in the parent's home but had daily contacts with the parent, and a home visit confirms no sleeping arrangements or toys for a child of appropriate age then the allegation might be true. An investigative study which did not include any contact with collaterals could easily result in an assessment that this particular parent had excellent parenting skills (based on answers in an interview) when in reality this parent was not even assuming the routine child care responsibilities for the child. The investigative worker must realize the importance of getting a total picture of a situation and not just focusing on one or two tasks in completing the investigative custody report.

An investigative worker needs to obtain relevant social and academic information from the children's school. Information should include the child's behavior, attitudes, academic abilities and achievement, observations concerning personal hygiene, and attendance. Also, it is relevant to obtain information concerning parental involvement in attending school conferences and activities as well as the parent's perceived attitudes toward their children's education.

An integral aspect of collateral investigation is checking and verifying each parent's employment, length of employment, and income. In some cases, where there appears to be a question, checking with past employers of parents may well be in order to determine reasons for termination and other important information regarding character.

Questions Used with Collaterals

1. Do you know both parties or each party involved in the current custody proceedings?
2. How long have you known each person?
3. What is the nature of your relationship or contacts with each person?
4. Have you had an opportunity to observe each person with the child or children involved in the custody litigation?
5. What are your observations?
6. What would you consider each litigant's strengths to be in terms of their parenting abilities?
7. What would you consider each litigant's weaknesses to be in terms of their parenting abilities?
8. Are there any additional direct concrete observations you have that would be beneficial to know in regard to either litigant's parenting abilities?
9. Are you aware of any problems either litigant has that would interfere with their ability to provide a home environment that would meet the physical, emotional, spiritual, medical, and/or educational needs of a child?

Additional questions may need to be asked, depending on the allegations in the petition, the information being given by the collateral, and the type of information expected by collaterals who are professionals. Additional questions are nearly always needed to clarify the exact nature of a collateral's observations of a litigant's relationship with a child (specifically the approximate date or dates of the collateral's contacts with the litigant and/or the child, amount of time the collateral spent in each observation, and the total number of relevant observations). It is important to know whether or not a collateral is related to one of the litigants as this may affect the perceptions of the collateral. It is essential that any allegation of medical neglect must include an interview or interviews with a physician as part of the investigative procedures.

Included in the appendices are additional forms for various collateral contacts, including: (1) collateral form (Appendix 24) (2) law enforcement form (Appendix 23) (3) verification of employment form (Appendix 25) and (4) school report form (Appendix 22).

Forms and Procedures

The forms and procedures mentioned in this chapter and in the appendices are all designed to provide a systematic objective investigation that will result in a thorough assessment of parenting abilities of litigants as well as an assessment of the Major and Minor Criteria listed in Chapter III. The forms and procedures are designed to provide consistency in format for each investigation and should result in markedly increased objectivity.

The forms and procedures are also designed to offer a logical step-by-step process that has proven to be helpful in arriving at a conclusion regarding which parent is better able to provide the most nurturing home environment for the child or children involved. Proceeding through each procedure listed and then reviewing all the written notes on interviews as well as any forms completed by parents, children, and/or collaterals all help to "fit the pieces of the puzzle together," obtaining as clear a picture as possible of each litigant's parenting abilities and home environment. Without all forms and procedures followed, the possibility increases that relevant information may be left out which might be vital in determining the conclusions and recommendations for custody.

In summary, it is important to utilize the forms and procedures in order to provide data that can be analyzed in the assessment phase of the investigation. The more relevant factual data that can be obtained prior to completion of the investigation, the more basis one can have for any conclusions regarding what would be in the best interests of the family.

Utilizing the Forms

Most of the forms included in the appendices come from *A Manual on Investigating Child Custody Reports*.[4] It is important that the litigants and children complete each form (with the exception of the basic data questionnaire) in the investigator's presence and that the forms not be sent by mail. It has been our experience that in many cases parents will have spouses complete the initial questionnaire (in cases where parents have remarried) or might consult with an attorney in attempts to obtain help or advice on the best way to answer each question. One particular parent had his attorney complete the questionnaire. The forms such as the Completion and True/False forms are utilized in helping to assess parenting abilities of parents as well as the Major and Minor Criteria. It is therefore very important that the investigator obtain each parent's own ideas and feelings. Using consistent methodology each parent also has the opportunity to complete the forms in the same standardized manner.

Be sure to have the children complete their own forms if they are old enough to do so. If not old enough or if a parent or child is not able to read or write, the questions may be read and the person's exact response to each question can be recorded on the forms. The professional completing the form should sign the form with a statement of the name of the person providing the answers, as well as the date and where the interview was conducted. It is important that the parents and children who complete their own forms sign their name on each form and write the date the form was completed.

The value of the above procedures cannot be overemphasized. For example, one parent testified in court that he assumed the majority of child care responsibilities himself during his marriage. When the author looked at the child care task form he completed during the investigation, his answers clearly indicated that he only assumed major child care responsibilities for one or two child care tasks listed and that his ex-wife assumed the majority of the child care responsibilities. Those particular child care task forms completed by the parents were entered as evidence at the court hearing. It is difficult for a parent to dispute his own answers to questions when confronted with the form he obviously completed.

Obviously, there are no "right" or "wrong" answers as such on the forms, and how one form or one or two questions are answered are not the most important considerations. However, the forms provide additional data that can be analyzed in their entirety, along with answers to interview questions, observations of interactions between each parent and child, information from collaterals, and all other data available that would be relevant in assessing the Major and Minor Criteria.

Whether or not the forms are answered truthfully can also be assessed. For example, if a litigant answers "false" to the question regarding whether he has ever had any problem with alcohol or drugs and then you have documentation that he has been diagnosed by mental health staff as being an alcoholic or has been in an inpatient alcoholic treatment program, there is a good possibility that the litigant's other answers to questions might not be answered honestly and that litigant's credibility would come into serious question.

Answers to questions on the forms that seem inappropriate should be discussed with the litigant during interviews to try to assess the reason for the answers. Inappropriate answers may be due to inappropriate child rearing philosophy, a lack of understanding of the meaning of the question, a matter of a litigant not reading the question carefully enough, or the litigant may have an explanation that would be appropriate within a certain context. For example, if a child says that he is being followed, it may sound like a possible symptom of paranoia when in fact a child might be followed by a parent or by a person such as a detective hired by one of the parents. Therefore, the child's statement that he is being followed might be very true and factual.

Answers to forms such as the child care task forms completed by litigants may be compared to a child's answers to the child care tasks form for comparison purposes. For example, if a mother indicates her husband virtually assumed no child care responsibilities but her husband and child both indicate that he was the primary person responsible for child care tasks during the marriage, then it would seem that the mother's answers may not be accurate. This would seem to be the case unless another explanation is available, such as the son being in fear of angering his father.

It should be emphasized that the forms are only one source of data utilized in the assessment phase and should be considered and reviewed in addition to all other data prior to completing the assessment.

The Home Visit

The home visit is an essential part of an investigation as it provides one of the best opportunities for the investigator to assess the following:

(1) the type of physical home environment provided by each litigant; (2) the presence or absence of health or safety hazards (particularly for infants or toddlers); (3) the interaction of a child with a parent in a more relaxed setting than an office or courtroom; (4) discipline techniques utilized by each parent as situations arise during the home visit which would warrant intervention by the parent; (5) the extent to which the home environment is child oriented or adult oriented; (6) the type of nutrition provided during a typical meal (if home visit is unannounced and at a time when a meal is being prepared or eaten; and (7) an assessment of the child's emotional state while in each environment. An attempt may be made to assess one or more of the above seven areas without a home visit, but the chances of obtaining a more accurate picture of each area is greatly enhanced by one or more actual home visits to each parent's home. There is no real substitute for first-hand observation of a home environment.

It should be emphasized that unless there are concerns regarding safety or health hazards to a child or a concern that a home environment results in neglect to a child, the physical environment is one of the *least* important aspects to consider in assessing the Major and Minor Criteria. The emotional relationship of each parent with the child, which parent provides the most nurturing environment, etc. is much more important than the physical environment. For example, it is generally better for a child to be in a nurturing environment provided by a parent who resides in a camper trailer than for the child to be in a mansion with a busy or neglectful parent.

It must be emphasized here that many parents will attempt to put on a good show during home visits which result in a very stilted and artificial visit. This type of visit is easily detected by noticing the level of spontaneity of the children during such a performance. The investigator should emphasize to the parents that natural and routine procedures should be the rule for such visits. On one such visit I experienced a father who had a prepared videotape of a "typical" family activity which he played for the investigator during the home visit.

Assessing Major and Minor Criteria

Assessing the Major and Minor Criteria takes several hours following the conclusion of the investigative process. The same criteria worksheet is used by the investigator as is used by the evaluator during this process.

The investigator should fill out the worksheet independently of the evaluator when there is Team involvement.

The Written Report

When litigants refuse an out-of-court settlement it is obligatory on the part of the investigator to write a separate report for the court, whether or not the investigator is working as part of a Team. The complete report to the court should include:

1. Completed questionnaires returned by the litigants
2. Interviews of litigants
3. Interviews of children (if 5 years or older)
4. Interviews of collaterals
5. Observations during home visits
6. Observations of children's interactions with each parent
7. Forms completed by litigants, children and/or relevant collaterals
8. Assessment of Major & Minor Criteria of each parent
9. Conclusion and recommendations

It should be noted that copies of the questionnaires completed by each litigant are included with the investigator's typed court report which routinely is sent to the appropriate judge as well as the attorneys involved in the case including the GAL. If a litigant does not have an attorney representing him, then, by law in Illinois, he or she is to be sent a copy of the court report directly.

Information Needed For Final Report to Court

Investigative Custody Report

1. Docket number.
2. County of court jurisdiction.
3. Each litigant's name and address.
4. Names and birthdates of the children involved in the custody proceedings.
5. Method utilized in completing Investigative Custody Report.
6. Worker's contacts with litigants.
7. Number of hours spent on investigation and how spent.
8. Contacts with collaterals.
9. Significant information obtained during interviews with children.

10. Significant information obtained during interviews with litigants (including allegations, if any).
11. Significant information obtained from collaterals.
12. Observations during home visits.
13. Observations of children's interaction with each litigant.
14. An assessment of parental strengths and weaknesses as they relate to the Major and Minor Criteria.
15. Conclusions and recommendations for custody and recommendations.
16. Copies of all forms by litigants, children, and collaterals.

Appendix 27 is an example of a completed investigative written report to the court. A normal investigative procedure appears to take fifteen to twenty hours to complete.

Meeting with the Team

The investigator is ready to meet with the other Team members when the Criteria Worksheet is prepared and prior to any formal written report to the court. The worksheets of both the evaluator and investigator are gone over, discussed, defended, and clarified until there is basic agreement on all the criteria. Again, in our experience when all Team members have done thorough and objective work, there is usually not much disagreement. A more detailed description of procedure at this point in the process is presented in Chapter 6.

Putting It Together Without a Team

If the investigator is involved in a custody case in which there is no evaluator, then the procedures would include the following:

1. Complete all procedures and methods advocated here as well as in *A Manual on Investigating Child Custody Reports*[4]
2. Complete a thorough assessment of the Major and Minor criteria in relation to each litigant.
3. Schedule an appointment to meet with the litigants jointly to discuss the results of the assessment and recommendations. Try to obtain an out-of-court settlement by the litigants and attorney representing the children if at all possible. The settlement can then be presented to the adversarial attorneys involved in the case for

their recommendations and advice. If it is not possible to reach an agreement, then the case can be scheduled for a court hearing and a final report to the court submitted.

Whether or not the investigator is completing the assessment alone or in conjunction with an evaluator, it is essential that the main focus is on the parenting abilities of litigants, the needs of the children, the Major and Minor criteria and what is in the best interests of the family and children. The assessment must be based on a thorough objective investigation and based on factual documentation that is consistent with the recommendations. The rationale behind the recommendations should be based on logical and specific documentation that could be justified in court if there is a need.

The ultimate goal of the investigator without involvement of an evaluator is still to explore the possibility of an out-of-court settlement being successfully agreed upon by the investigator, litigants, and guardian-ad-litem after the investigation has been completed. There is a greater possibility of out-of-court settlements becoming more common in the future if custody investigators have the specialized knowledge, expertise, experience, and skills to be able to facilitate resolving custody conflicts without adversarial court proceedings.

Litigants, investigators, judges, attorneys, and most importantly, the children in the middle of contested custody litigation can all reap the benefits of professional input from custody specialists. There is much to gain in routinely utilizing the ethics, methods, and procedures advocated in this book, not only in Illinois, but in other states as well.

Chapter VI

TAKING CHARGE: THE TEAM'S PREPARATION AND MEETING WITH THE PARENTS

Differences Between the Family's Team Procedure and Mediation/Arbitration

Mediation and arbitration are generally excellent methods for helping families resolve both marital and child custody issues. While there has been much resistance to these methods by the legal profession in the past, the contemporary legal trend in family law is toward mediation and arbitration. Mediation is a process whereby a neutral party assists two opposing parties in resolving their differences. Generally the mediation process encourages the parties to take the major problem-solving role themselves. Nonbinding arbitration differs from mediation in that the arbitrator assumes a more central and powerful role as he or she is asked to provide specific recommendations to the parties. Unlike the adversarial method, the emphasis in mediation and arbitration is not upon "right and wrong" or "bad and good," but rather on achieving a resolution of conflict through compromise which meets everyone's needs to some extent. For more detailed descriptions of mediation and arbitration see Chapter 7 in Gardner.[1]

The Family's Team approach includes much of what is positive and humane in mediation and arbitration. It is closest to arbitration in that the Team can provide specific recommendations; however, like mediation, the parents are encouraged and supported to settle the matter of custody and visitation themselves. Rather than adversarily disempowering parents, thus risking psychopathology and lowered self-esteem, the Team promotes the empowerment of parents based upon detailed information and state of the art criteria. The major additions to mediation and arbitration methodology provided by the Family's Team approach include:

1. A very detailed and objectively based evaluation and investigation of all potential litigants and significant collaterals.
2. Sensitive evaluation of and input from the children involved in the

custody matter by mental health experts aided by a legal representative for the children and/or the family.
3. Use of clear, up-to-date major and minor criteria for recommendations.
4. Detailed and specific research aided recommendations as to custody, visitation, and future mental health needs.

The Team's Meeting

Following separate evaluation and investigation, the Team members meet to go over their results, conclusions, and to formulate their recommendations to the parents. It is our experience that in the dozen or so cases in which the authors worked together, we have never failed to agree on custody recommendations. In most cases there should be little confusion on the part of mental health professionals when they have done a thorough job. When the Criteria Worksheets and recommendations of the Team have been finalized, a final Criteria Worksheet (Appendix 1) is filled out reflecting the decisions and rationale for each major and minor criterion. This worksheet is then copied and provided to the parents and their attorneys.

At this point the Team should be prepared to meet with the parents in an attempt to arbitrate an out-of-court settlement.

The Parent and Team Meeting

The senior mental health professional should be in charge of the actual meeting of parents and Team whenever possible.

Following is a minimum list of topic areas to be included in this crucial meeting:

1. Provide parents with a written copy of Criteria Worksheet and recommendations, including visitation with noncustodial parent.
2. A clear statement of parental legal rights, especially that the parents do not have to abide by the team's recommendations.
3. A restatement of our philosophy that children develop more optimally when there is little or no conflict between their divorced parents regardless of who has custody; that it is ordinarily not so crucial to the children who has custody as it is *how* the parents

relate to each other and the children following the marital breakup and resolution of custody.

4. Give the parents an invitation to correct any factual information or opinions based upon false information contained in the Criteria Worksheet.

5. Inform the parents that any agreements reached during this meeting are not binding and they should seek advice of counsel prior to any final, out-of-court agreement.

6. Further educate the parents concerning potential damage to themselves and their children from prolonged adversarial litigation. Any information given in this regard should be specific, as the Team should now know each individual and their particular vulnerabilities. For example, to the parents of a sudden underachiever in school, the clinician might say, "You have observed that Johnnie has begun to say hateful and exaggerated things about his father and has begun to do poorly in school. What do you folks think is underlying this change?" From there you can have an insightful dialogue about loyalty conflicts and the potential insidiousness of Parent Alienation Syndrome (see Chapter VIII).

7. Go over each recommendation with the parents allowing them flexibility to modify within reason. Unreasonable demands or guilt induced concessions should be met with strong confrontation and rational explanation. For example, the more financially advantaged parent may attempt to exert undue influence on a more needy spouse in an effort to gain equal time with the children. When equal time is clearly not to the developmental advantage of the children, this must be strongly pointed out to the parent with appropriate data from developmental psychology. Also, parents who are pathologically motivated by guilt and masochistic tendencies may wish to turn over total control of the children to the ex-spouse without even visitation. This, too, must be met with strong confrontation by the Team, including an explanation of children's needs and advantages of having two active and strong parents.

8. Give the parents warning that should they allow a third party (e.g., the judge) to determine custody, that there is increased danger that they could well be regularly returning to court for modification of custody until the children are adults. This danger is reduced if the

parents or guardians themselves make the necessary compromises and decisions.
9. Finally, facilitate a discussion among the parents geared toward a resolution of the custody and visitation dilemma. For example, after much explanation and discussion, the Team leader states, "Well, you have the recommendations and the rationale behind them. Which one of you is willing to offer a proposal to the other," or "Well, there you have our input. Does this sound reasonable enough for you both to live with?"

It is the Team's task during this meeting to help the parents focus on the relevant issues in a cooperative, problem-solving manner. If the facilitation of the meeting is weak, the parents will get sidetracked on nonresolvable, competitive issues rather than dealing with what is best for their broken family. For example, one stepmother in an unconscious attempt to induce guilt in this evaluator and divert attention from a recommendation that her spouse remove all guns from his home during the children's visits, righteously insisted that I was calling her a liar because I tended to believe the adolescent's story concerning her husband's alleged manipulation of the children with a gun (he had allegedly held a gun to his own head and threatened to kill himself in front of the children). She continued her indignant insistence that I was calling her a liar because, "If you believe him (the adolescent male), then you're calling me a liar!" I repeatedly pointed out to her that whether or not she was a liar was not the issue, that the issue was how to safely and effectively reestablish a relationship between a father and his children with whom her husband had lost positive, emotional contact. It would be of benefit to the Team to have at least one member with mediation and/or arbitration training. One of the Team members should keep notes regarding any verbal agreements made by the parents in this session. At the end of the session, any agreements should be carefully read back to the parents for their approval. If approval is obtained for an out-of-court settlement, the parents are instructed to contact their attorneys and the Team will send a copy of the agreement to their respective counsel for their scrutiny and any appropriate legal action. All attorneys should have been prepared for the possibilities of an out-of-court settlement from the beginning.

Team and Family meetings should not exceed 2½ hours. At times an additional meeting is needed and should be so arranged. If one or both parents are not willing to settle, they need to be informed that a full report by the evaluator and the investigator will be sent to the court and each attorney with the stated recommendations for custody and visitation.

It has been our experience that most refusals of an out-of-court settlement are motivated either by righteous indignation in an effort to cover up deep feelings of inadequacy and low self-esteem or by the need to "save face" in the immediate situation. In any situation where a parent refuses settlement, we nonjudgmentally support that parent's right and leave the door open to future negotiation up to and including trial day settlement in the judge's chambers. A power struggle with the resistant parent(s) at this juncture would be an error that could make it impossible for a future out of court settlement.

Parental Righteousness—"The Golden Chain"

According to Buddhist doctrine, the final gate which prohibits entering into the state of Nirvana is called the "golden chain." The "golden chain" refers to self-righteousness. Self-righteousness is the unmitigated insistence that one is right and thereby good and the other is wrong and consequently bad or even evil. Due to several factors including our culture's competitive and blaming nature, the either/or quality of the adversarial legal system and the esteem laden issue of "possession" of children, it is most usual for parents and others vying for custody and visitation rights to become extremely self-righteous and quite hostile. The task of the Team members in handling their hostility is not an easy one and is not for the fainthearted. Where attorneys are quite accustomed to such negativity, most mental health workers are not. It is imperative that Team members keep their psychological boundaries (a sense of who they are and what they are doing) else risk getting lost in the confusion of guilt, uncertainty, and defensiveness when confronted with parental righteousness. From the example of the irate stepmother earlier, it should be clear to the reader what could have happened to the problem-solving process had the evaluator become defensively engaged in her diversionary maneuver. Becoming defensive presents a dual dilemma to the whole concept of humanistic problem solving. First of all, defensiveness can lead to inadvertently appeasing the offended party thus compromising the entire family, especially the relatively helpless children. Secondly, defensiveness can promote our own self-righteousness and we can overtly or covertly punish the offending party further by becoming stubbornly fixated on our being "right," once again compromising the family and the children, consequently "losing the forest for the trees." I am reminded of the poignant insight given by Sheldon Kopp in his book, *The Pickpocket and the Saint.*[5] Kopp reminds us that whenever we directly or indirectly punish our clients it is because their behavior is making it quite difficult for us to maintain our own secret, grandiose sense of ourselves.

So, how do we handle these often verbally violent attacks on our sense of ourselves? The solutions are simple, but not easy:

1. Remember the central issue of the evaluation which is to determine what is in the best interest of the family. The central issue is not who is right, wrong, bad, or good.

2. Accept with genuine understanding the feelings, attitudes, and behavior of all parties. That is not to say deny inappropriate attitudes and behavior, but rather use them as data in an objective, nonpunitive manner in an attempt to offer the parties expanded self-awareness and rationale for your conclusions and recommendations.

3. Always bring the focus of attention back to the central issues when the parties stray into self-righteousness or other tangential topics. For example, to a mother fixated on her ex-husband's morality and violence, "I understand, Mrs. Jones, that your husband ran around on you and has beaten you. If this is true, it certainly says something about his character; nevertheless, your relationship with him was and is separate from his relationship with the children and we need to try and work out what is in everyone's best interest today. Especially we need to realize that children have a legal right and a psychological need to have a relationship with both parents. Perhaps you could ask him now if he intends to physically punish the children when he is responsible for them..."

4. In clearly extreme cases it is necessary to appropriately warn parents that continuation of their hostile attitudes could seriously threaten their hoped for outcome. For example, the evaluator might say to an extremely agitated father or mother whose hostility is out of control, "Should you continue your hostile behavior toward me and your ex-spouse, this could have serious consequences for the outcome of this evaluation. Are you in agreement that the children need a conflict free relationship with both of their parents?"

5. In some extreme cases when one or both parents stubbornly utilize the evaluation and problem-solving process to continue their marital battle, it may be best for Team members to have separate meetings with each parent. In this way each parent can be invited out of the competitive arena and away from the old marital conflict. This method gives the parents a chance to "come up for air" and gain some perspective

and self-awareness. During these individual sessions it is important to stay focused on the relevant issues and bring the parent back to these issues when he or she strays into blaming and complaining. Often in these individual sessions I will nonjudgmentally talk about how that parent seems to have hurt the other party and suggest that when we come together again that he or she genuinely apologize and offer to "bury the hatchet." When this invitation is met with continued resistance and hostility, I often offer the litigant the age old wisdom that, "If you do not recognize and learn from your mistakes, then you are doomed to repeat them."

Regardless of efforts, sometimes we get nowhere in our repetitive attempts to assist parents to drop their self-righteousness and focus on what is relevant. When this is the case, we state this information strongly in our reports and this greatly affects the major criteria of psychological parenting, flexibility, and emotional stability of the offending party.

Verbal and Written Agreements

When the Team's efforts prevail and the parents are willing to come to an agreement, we generally do the following:

1. Prior to leaving the meeting, the Team reads each point of agreement to correct any errors and change wording for the sake of clarity and precision.
2. Once the agreement is acceptable we inform the parents that this is not as yet a binding agreement. They should first consult their respective attorneys to be sure their rights are protected. We inform the parents that we will immediately send their attorneys a copy of the unofficial agreement.
3. We inform the parents that unless something unforeseen happens, this will be the last contact we will have. The attorneys should be able to negotiate and file any necessary legal documents.
4. We advise the parents that there may be family and friends who will not understand the decisions they have made because they were not a part of the problem-solving process. We encourage them to stand firm in the fact of others' disappointment and attack by remembering the relevant issues. We remind them that their friends and family may still be caught in an adversarial and competitive nightmare which would prolong the despair, hatred, and vindictiveness causative of adult and child psychopathology.
5. One member of the Team takes responsibility for the immediate

typing and copying of the agreement and sending it to the parents' attorneys. Any further contact with the Team members should generally be made by the attorneys and not the parents. This is done to help insure objectivity and prevent a resumption of parental competitiveness.

6. Any contact by Team members with the parents' attorneys should be made, if possible, by conference call. This prevents the seeding of paranoia which can germinate into future conflict and a resumption of the competition between the parents. When it is necessary to converse with just one of the adversarial attorneys and a conference call is not possible, a letter to that attorney, with a copy to the other attorney is appropriate. Often this method creates a need for a phone call to explain the background and circumstances of the letter. When this is not possible, a letter to one attorney stating what has transpired is crucial. The Team's integrity and objectively must not be compromised. A sample of a nonbinding parental agreement sent to attorneys can be found in Appendix 26.

Chapter VII

VISITATION

The Problem

Even more than arriving at custody recommendations, the task of providing visitation guidelines is extremely sensitive. More than any other aspect of custody evaluation, visitation guidelines serve as the breeding ground of continued and prolonged litigation long after the original custody dispute is resolved. There are precious few visitation guidelines which are based upon solid research. In addition, the Team must carefully analyze not only the quality of parenting ability of the litigants, but must also assess their potential for continued conflict once the basic custody decision is made. For many parents the end of the custody battle signals the beginning of a prolonged psychological power struggle which can seriously affect the quality of the children's lives. For this reason, the Team approach calls for vigorous attempts to assist the parents themselves in defining the visitation patterns. In addition to having no basis in fact or research, the every other weekend pattern prescribed by many judges in adversarial court further alienates the litigants from the system and from each other by rendering them powerless in the critical decisions affecting their children's as well as their own lives. This sense of powerlessness and helplessness causes much unnecessary psychopathology and irresponsible behavior in even the most healthy of individuals. This approach of empowering the parents is in line with our second ethical principle of maintaining the integrity of the family without undue interference from outside sources.

Ideal Visitation

Ideal visitation is a pattern of visitation which the parents choose themselves and which takes into account the developmental needs of children at their current age. Ideal visitation is flexible and takes into account the changing needs of children as well as the changing circumstances of the parents. Too many parents who leave all the decisions to the "powers-that-be" or to experts maintain such rigidity that they cannot adjust from the time guidelines even should a set of grandparents drop in unexpectedly at the former spouse's home. If it is not the visitation weekend, the children simply do not go.

Judicial Dilemma

More than any other aspect of custody, visitation disputes cause repetitive chronic litigation for the courts. Most judges have little patience with these chronic disputes, yet there is little they can do to resolve them. Judges are also human and have extreme difficulty in determining who to believe and what to do, even if they do believe one party more than the other. In addition, if judges are to punish one party by reducing visitation for irresponsibility, is that not punishing the children for the sins of the parents? Judges do not have an enviable task in this type of chronic litigation. It is generally true that flexible and frequent visitation with the noncustodial parent is healthy for most children. It is imperative that litigating parties be educated toward this end which includes educating them that judges are not omnipotent, nor do the courts have much capacity to supervise their own decisions.

Evaluating Parents for Visitation

The Team approach to visitation is generally to assist the parents to make decisions themselves. The most predictive measure of future conflict in visitation is found in the Major Criteria which deal with Emotional Stability (#3) of each parent and especially Parental Flexibility (#5). Borrowing a term from Hodges,[2] the concepts of High Quality/Low Conflict parenting styles is extremely useful. It is the Team's task to assess the litigants on the following continuiums:

Low Quality . . . . . . High Quality
High Conflict . . . . . . Low Conflict

The following operational definitions of these terms are offered which are reflective of the authors', not Hodges' use of these concepts:

Low Quality Parenting

A low quality parenting style is characterized by rigidity, defensiveness, and lack of psychological insight into their children's needs as well as their own behavior. Parents who fit this category cannot tell you their weaknesses, but rather focus on the flaws and weaknesses of the other parent or litigant. Often parents who are or have been sexually, physically, or emotionally abusive fit this category. Also parents who are chemically dependent may well fit this category as their dependency needs usually come before the child's needs. Rather than list all the possible specific symptoms of low quality parenting, the authors advise that an objective analysis of parental defensiveness, rigidity, and psychological insight be conducted regardless of the particular symptomological form it takes. Typical examples of low quality parenting include spending almost no time with the children in activities, sexual or physical abuse of children, continually denigrating the children's other parent in their presence, drug and/or alcohol abuse, lack of affection, setting poor or no limits on children's behavior, setting extremely rigid and inappropriate limits on children, chronically blaming others, etc.

High Quality Parenting

This type of parenting is characterized by openness, honesty, and insight. Such parents can openly acknowledge their weaknesses as well as their strengths. They own responsibility for their own feelings, thoughts, and behavior rather than blaming others as low quality parents do. Such parents expect age appropriate behavior from their children and neither infantalize them nor parentify them. Such parents allow their children freedom to express their feelings and to disagree with them without the children feeling threatened by inappropriate retaliation.

High Conflict Parenting

This type of parenting is characterized by chronic fault-finding and blaming of others, especially the other parent. Such parents tend to be caught up in moral righteousness and knowingly or unknowingly use the children and the entire custody/visitation dispute as a soapbox to attack the other litigant and prove a point. Such parents are the kind that refuse to grant visitation due to a late child support payment or because the former spouse now has a lover. Such parents continually find reason to use the children in a punishing manner toward the other parent. A sure sign of a high conflict parent is the current trend of continually reporting unfounded abuse or neglect charges to children and family services agencies. In most custody cases the parents have been separated for some length of time and the children have been in the temporary custody of one of the parents. An assessment of any conflict regarding visitation during this period is usually predictive of future difficulty unless the parent(s) genuinely gain insight into their manipulative behaviors and decide to change.

Low Conflict Parenting

This type of parenting is reflected in the parents' support of the other litigant and their recognition of the importance of that relationship to the children. Because a parent may be high quality does not alone mean that the parent is also low conflict. We have seen many high quality parents who have such unresolved resentment toward their former spouse that they become extremely conflictual when having to deal with them over any issue involving the children. When high quality parenting is carried over into negotiations regarding the children with the former spouse, you have an ideal framework from which to assist litigants in negotiating optimal visitation schedules.

Most of the information needed by the Team in evaluating parents for visitation has been gathered in the formal custody evaluation, especially when assessing the Major and Minor Criteria. It should not be difficult in reframing that information for use in visitation negotiations.

It should be kept in mind during these negotiations that the purpose of the entire Team's approach is to reduce conflict and consequent stress on the entire family, especially the children. Children do not function optimally under stress. This fact should be repeated as often as necessary to the litigants. We have had several children with courage enough to tell their parents in an evaluation session to "please cut it out" (e.g., the fighting) because they couldn't stand it. It does not matter much to most healthy children if one of their parents is right or not. What matters most to them is to get relief from the stress of the family breakup and from their parents' adversarial attitudes and behavior.

Visitation Recommendations When There Is High Quality, Low Conflict Parenting

Unfortunately, this is a rather rare occurrence in our experience; nevertheless, there are some parents who fit this category. With such parents the Team's task is simply to provide information to them. Most of this information comes from Hodges' excellent guidelines on visitation and access. Needed information includes developmental needs of the children at their current age, information on the memory capacities of children at certain ages, guidelines on frequency of visitation, demographic considerations when appropriate, the need for flexibility, and the changing needs and desires of children as they mature. Working with such parents it is our experience that our main task is simply to point out if an aspect of their visitation plan is not a sound one due to the developmental needs of the children. For example, if the parents of a six-month-old infant want to split the time between houses we would point out the needs of the child to have a familiar and stable physical environment until the child gets older.

As a final recommendation to even High Quality, Low Conflict parents, we advise them that should unresolvable disagreements come about regarding the children that they consult an appropriate mental health expert rather than returning to litigation.

Visitation Recommendations When There Is Low Quality, High Conflict or High Quality, High Conflict Parenting

In our experience this is the most common occurrence in litigated custody dilemmas. Unfortunately, visitation recommendations in such cases need to be more concrete, definitive and less flexible. Such recommendations generally take the form of arbitration where the Team specifically defines the recommendations and the litigants are given copies and then assisted in negotiation based upon the Team's recommendations. The following factors need to be explained to the parents:

1. Age and developmental needs of children.
2. Memory capacity of children (e.g., Young children have less developed memory capacity and can more quickly forget who a parent is).
3. Explanation of visitation frequency recommendations.
4. Demographic considerations (when applicable).

5. An explanation of the child's need for uncomplicated and uninterrupted contact with the noncustodial parent.
6. Guidelines and recommendations for change in visitation at various developmental milestones. Often we make a strong recommendation for reevaluation of visitation by an expert at the next developmental milestone. For example, the overriding need of children under 18 months is for continuity of care and affection. Because of this, we may recommend two to five, one- or two-hour visits with the noncustodial parent during the week, but no overnights. When the child reaches 18 to 36 months of age, we would meet again and likely recommend beginning overnight visitation.
7. Strong education of the parents as to the needs and benefits of nonconflictual visitation with the noncustodial parent. Hodges'[2] recommendations on visitation contain an excellent outline of the foundations for visitation including:
    A. Visitation agreements must protect the rights of the child for access to the noncustodial parent.
    B. Visitation agreements must protect the right of the noncustodial parent.
    C. Visitation agreements must insure that the emotional bond of the child with both parents is protected.
    D. Visitation provides the custodial parent with relief from the parenting role.
    E. Visitation provides alternative role models for the child.
8. Such high conflict parents need to be taught some basic information about psychological boundaries and children's loyalty conflicts. Specifically, the parents need to gain the insight that the other parent's relationship with each child is separate and different from their own relationship with the child.
9. Such parents are extremely competitive and are often easily hurt and angered by the natural flow of attachment from one parent to another over time. They should be educated that this flow is normal and is not necessarily a result of "brainwashing" by the other parent.
10. Such parents should be given handouts and literature with as much information as possible concerning single parenting, visitation problems, relevant childhood development, and other appropriate materials.

11. In some cases, family, couples, or individual counseling should be recommended in an effort to reduce the stress regarding custody and visitation.

Some of the teachings for handling self-righteousness discussed in Chapter IV are usually helpful in making visitation recommendations to high conflict parents. Additionally, it is often helpful to utilize the technique of role reversal with such parents. Role reversal involves inviting each parent into the child's role and asking them what they would like from each of their parents. Often this can lead to profound insight and a lessening of the conflict between the parents.

During this phase which occurs during the Teams' meeting with the parents described in Chapter VI, it is important that the Team take careful notes and keep an accurate record on what agreements the litigants make. If settled out of court, these agreements need to be sent to the parties' attorneys for translation into appropriate legalese for court approval. In cases where the parents refuse to settle out of court, the attitudes and behavior of the parents during this phase of the assessment can be invaluable data in supporting the Team's visitation recommendations to the court.

General Visitation Guidelines by Age and Development

The following guidelines are primarily the result of the invaluable work done by Hodges.[2] A review of Hodges' book is strongly recommended to professionals who work in the area of custody and visitation.

0 to 6 months: Frequent and predictable visitation. Infants should spend more time with custodial parent. Visits of one to two hours every day or every other day are optimal. No overnight visits are recommended. Eating and sleeping arrangements should be stable.

6 to 18 months: Short visits of one to three hours recommended if visits are infrequent (one per week or less). If visits are more frequent, the length of visit can vary according to parental needs. Visitation should be in the child's home as overnight visits are still not recommended. Exceptions to this can be made if geographic distance precludes the recommended frequent visitation. Such long distance visits should be made only in conjunction with advice and guidelines supplied by a children's mental health professional.

18 months to 3 years: Such "toddlers" can handle less visitation and still maintain bonding with a noncustodial parent. Overnight visits are now recommended; however, not for an entire weekend or for an extended period in the summer. When geographic distance is a factor, the noncustodial parent should travel to the child's location if at all possible.

3 to 5 years: Such children need highly predictable visits. Weekend and extended time visits are recommended when there is high quality, low conflict parenting by the parents as long as these visits are not frequent (e.g., every other weekend is generally acceptable for this age group). If visits last more than a week, contact should be maintained with the custodial parent during this time.

6 to 10 years: If high quality, low conflict parenting exists visitation for more than the usual every other weekend, every other holiday and six weeks in the summer is desirable. Liberal visits for seven to ten year olds during the week is correlated in the research with contentment of children. During this stage children can benefit more from contact with a noncustodial parent than at other developmental stages. If conflict between parents is high, a predictable, structured visitation schedule is preferable. Long visits are helpful, but contact with the custodial parent needs to be maintained during such visits.

11 to 13 years: Such children should have some say in visitation, particularly in high quality, low conflict situations. Boys tend to prefer less contact at this age and should be permitted less contact (e.g., every other week rather than weekly) if they desire. Parents should be informed that the reason for this lessening of interest by children is often because of a normal, enhanced involvement with peers, not because of any "brainwashing."

Adolescents: Unless there are extreme circumstances such as Parent Alienation Syndrome, sexual or physical abuse, or the presence of a severe mental disorder to a parent, such children should be permitted to decide their own visitation. At this age adolescents do not need extended contact with either parent as their peer group and outside interests are paramount to their normal development. Expected contact with the available noncustodial parent is usually about once or twice a week for short durations (e.g., one to three hours). The primary difficulty adolescents have with visitation is feeling guilty should the noncustodial parent exhibit inappropriate displeasure to the adolescent due to decreased interest in visitation.

Generally speaking these guidelines are not "written in granite." Much more research needs to be done so that professionals can assist in such problems with more assurance. Nevertheless, these guidelines do represent current "state of the art" theory and research.

Special Considerations in Visitation

The "Santa Claus" Effect: Typically the noncustodial parent at the beginning of visitation will treat the children as though they were honored guests in his/her home, showering the children with gifts, affection, and other forms of special treats which, while the family was intact, was never evidenced. This is known as the "Santa Claus" effect. Often the family has been separated with one or the other of the parents having had temporary custody prior to the Team's evaluation. This effect must be kept in mind by the Team as children often show preferences for the "Santa Claus" parent. Parents should be warned of this behavior as it tends to feed the conflict between the parents and has consequent effect on the loyalty feelings and consequent stability of the children.

Grandparents' Visitation: In most states grandparents have gained legal rights to visitation with their grandchildren. In high quality, low conflict situations this is generally not a problem. In high conflict situations the noncustodial grandparents in many cases may literally never see the grandchildren. This is, indeed, a shame as a healthy relationship with grandparents can greatly enhance a child's life. A careful analysis of the quality and conflict between the parents is necessary in order to make such visitation recommendations. In some cases grandparent visitation can add fuel to the fire of already severely loyalty conflicted children. If such visitation appears to be an issue during the evaluation, it behooves the Team to invite the grandparents to a session in order to assess their level of conflict and to educate them to be properly supportive to both parents and the children.

Change of Lifestyle: When one parent remarries, especially the noncustodial parent, this can lead to a serious emotional conflict in some children. This is especially true in high conflict parents who have a legal, but not a psychological divorce from each others. Parents should be advised to seek joint mental health assistance with the child in such situations and to cooperate with the counselor for the sake of the children. Also, in some cases one parent may change his or her lifestyle to include homosexuality or bisexuality. This kind of change often induces severe tension and anxiety in the other parent and can lead to severe conflict concerning custody and/or visitation. Team recommendations regarding this issue often include counseling for the anxiety ridden parent and some reassurances that their ex-spouse's behavior does not automatically make their children homosexuals or bisexuals. We do caution the nonheterosexual parent that their children can suffer painful shame and humiliation from their peers due to his or her sexual preferences and advise that he or she take this into account when embarking on their nontraditional lifestyle. Such parents should proceed with caution concerning with whom and how they entertain while their children are present until the children are old enough to discuss and work through this potential problem area. Self-righteous parents need to be cautioned about the potential negative effects upon their children should they openly and publicly denounce the children's father or mother for their sexual preferences. In most, if not all states, homosexual and bisexual parents have the same legal rights to their children as do heterosexual parents. Sexual preference is ordinarily not a grounds for custody change or restricted visitation unless it can be shown under the rules of evidence that the sexual preference is endangering the child's physical health or significantly impairing the child's emotional development.

Supervised Visitation: Such visitations are extremely difficult and cumbersome for all involved. They should be avoided if at all possible. However, there are cases when a parent is so severely emotionally disturbed or such a threat to the child (such as a parent having been sexually or physically abusive to the child) that if contact with that parent is deemed necessary or desirable, it should be under supervision of a responsible adult. For example, it is important in the treatment of sexually abused children and their perpetrator parent to attend counseling sessions together in an attempt to reconcile the relationship as well as make it safe for the child to be with that parent in the future. The authors are constantly amazed at how some agencies and courts become so outraged at sexual abuse that they attempt to sever parent-child relationships forever without ever giving a thought to the healing of that relationship being in the child's best interest. On a television show during the last election campaign, Dan Quayle was being interviewed by a very bright 11–13 year old school reporter. She questioned him hypothetically concerning what her options should legally be should she become pregnant by a sexually abusing father. When Quayle replied that in his view she should have the baby, the reporter outlined the realistic consequences of this choice including missing school, being subject to the ridicule of her peers, and placing her physical health in jeopardy as she was not yet fully physically developed. Quayle's rather limp response was that essentially the system would take care of her including providing her with counseling and *breaking off all contact with her father*. The motivation for this severe stance against family perpetrators appears to be more to self-righteously appease individuals or to manipulate circumstances such as custody or material aspects of divorce than it is to understand what is in the best interests of families and children. Consequently, it is critical that cases which call for supervised visitation be carefully analyzed also from the point of view of the child before recommending a course of action.

Reducing Visitation Problems

It is always the Team's aim not only to serve as unbiased evaluators, but also to serve therapeutically, especially in the prevention of future psychological and physical harm to children and their parents. Following are some guidelines and strategies to prevent recurring problems and chronic litigation regarding visitation:

1. In high conflict litigants who show little or no promise of insight and change, it is necessary to be very detailed and specific concerning dates, times, pick up and delivery, location of exchange, child support payments, and any other behaviors which could set off a tug of war with the children cast in the role of the rope.
2. As much as possible lead the parents to their own conclusions as to what visitation schedule best serves the children's needs.
3. Whenever possible inject some humor into the proceedings. Litigants who can healthily laugh at themselves are less likely to get on a righteous bandwagon.
4. Give specific information as to why a specific visitation suggestion is made. Remember this is a competitive culture and parents are very sensitive to any hint of favoritism toward the other parent.
5. Give lots of praise whenever one or both parents are being cooperative or sensitive to the children's needs.
6. Provide parents with resources other than attorneys and court if problems with visitation should arise in the future.
7. Make appropriate counseling recommendations to parents, especially when it is apparent that they still have not worked through

their old marital resentments and pain. Even though the parents may have a legal divorce, it is still appropriate in many cases to recommend couples counseling should it be in the children's best interests. A legal divorce can be obtained very quickly. A psychological divorce typically takes years.

8. Probably most difficult of all is to maintain compassion for both sides throughout the process. These individuals have been constantly suffering criticism and self-doubt. Should you take sides or become angry and frustrated you will simply become a part of the problem, not the solution.

Chapter VIII

SPECIAL PROBLEMS IN CUSTODY EVALUATIONS AND INVESTIGATIONS

Parent Alienation Syndrome

Gardner has introduced a new concept into the field of custody decision making, the Parent Alienation Syndrome. The identification and defining of this syndrome is perhaps the most profound addition to custody literature since *Beyond the Best Interests of the Child*.[2] No one performing custody investigations or evaluations should be without a thorough understanding of this syndrome as it appears to some degree in nearly all cases. Defined by Gardner,[1] Parent Alienation Syndrome (PAS) is defined as:

> "a disturbance in which children are preoccupied with depreciation and criticism of a parent—denigration that is unjustified and/or exaggerated.

The ever increasing incidence of this disorder since the late 1970s appears to be a reflection of changing custody criteria in the courts as well as an outcome of an ever increasing competitive and litigious society. In the 1970s the judiciary began realizing that the "tender years presumption" by which a mother was nearly always superior to a father as a parent was inherently sexist. The courts began developing criteria which were more related to parenting ability than to the sex of a parent. This fact, along with a rising of male consciousness as child caretakers, has resulted in more men petitioning for custody. This new trend created a much more difficult, if not impossible task for the courts. Now we have more parents fighting with each other over custody, more ambiguous guidelines, and more attorneys entering the scene with their obligation, if not sometimes compulsion, to win at any cost. Literature began to appear which was geared to assisting fathers in "winning" custody of their children, e.g., *Winning Custody—A No-Holds-Barred Guide for Fathers*.[7] Currently, if you happen to visit a courtroom during a typical custody trial, it would be difficult to differentiate this civil, family matter from a criminal proceeding.

Due to these changes, which began in the 1970s, parents, especially mothers, are "brainwashing" their children more and more frequently and deeply in order to regain advantage and custody. While "brainwashing" is not the only component causative of PAS, it is often the most dominant factor. "Brainwashing" is the conscious or unconscious act of programming a child against one of the parents. "Brainwashing" has many obvious and extremely subtle variations. One parent may call the other parent names such as "adulterer," "whore," "druggie," "pervert," "alcoholic" etc. in front of the children. Quite common is when the mother expresses to the children regarding financial support the father is providing, "If your father really loved you, he wouldn't be so stingy!" While these are examples of some of the more obvious "brainwashing" techniques, some more sophisticated and vindictive parents are much more subtle. Some parents have "lovingly" brought their children to counseling because of the effects of the other parent's "abandonment" of the children or because of the "obvious" effects upon the children of that parent's alleged alcoholism or drug addiction. When evaluating such caring appearing behaviors it is critical that the expert assess the motivation for the behavior, not just take the behavior at face value. While in many cases it is a sign of good parenting to get their children counseling through such a trauma, if done for the wrong reasons it can inflict further damage. We have been involved in an ever increasing number of cases when a parent has repeatedly called the Department of Children and Family Services with unfounded abuse and neglect reports. In such cases the child is exposed to interrogation and is "smart" enough to say what he or she knows the "brainwashing" parent wants them to say.

For a more thorough description of how PAS is formed it is essential to read Gardner.[6] What does PAS look like? Often the "red flag" occurs when a child who is being evaluated is obsessed with the hatred of one of the parents. There is nothing good that they say about that parent and nothing bad that they can say about the so-called "preferred" parent. Often, even prior to any prompting, the child will delve into a diatribe of complaints about the so-called "hated" parent. Often their speech will have a rehearsed quality, including using words and concepts not typical of children, e.g., "My father has abandoned us" or "My father is not being financially responsible" or "My mother is a whore." This deluge of negativity is usually not restricted to the "hated" parent, but also toward that parent's family as well. Often there is evidence of a good prior relationship with grandparents, uncles and aunts, but now that custody is at issue the child speaks hatefully of these formerly enjoyed relationships.

Perhaps the key symptom in PAS is the child's almost or entire lack of ambivalence. Most children will be able to provide both positive and negative aspects of each of their parents or at least defensively state, "I don't know" when asked for good and bad points about their parents. Not so with children suffering from PAS. There is no such ambivalence. One parent is good and the other is bad.

Concerning this syndrome Gardner[6] states that should these symptoms remain in effect for over a year there is the strong likelihood that any meaningful relationship between the child and the "hated" parent is impossible until, at least, the child becomes an adult. This is quite a serious consequence and PAS must always be assessed in any competent custody evaluation or investigation. Gardner[6] further suggests to us that unless measures are taken to change the adversarial nature of settling custody disputes, that PAS will occur with more and more frequency along with its devastating destruction to relationships and children's character and development.

The incredible irony of PAS according to Gardner[6] is that most often the child's true feelings are quite the opposite to what is expressed through PAS. That is, it is more likely that the "preferred" parent is in reality more feared than preferred. And consequently, the "hated" parent is more loved than hated. Quite often the child's extreme response is more the result of the child being parentified to take care of the feelings of the "preferred" parent. Another term for this parentification process is reverse symbiosis. The child feels as though his or her last chance of survival is in the taking care of a parent's needs and feelings rather than the usual secure experience of the parent taking care of the child's feelings.

It should be remembered by the Team or individual evaluator that all custody conflicts include some "brainwashing" by both parents. Some PAS symptoms may occur without a full blown, pathological PAS. A careful analysis and judgment of the symptoms is necessary before deciding on recommendations. The inexperienced evaluator or investigator should seek consultation prior to forming conclusions. In addition, it is imperative that all professionals who deal with custody read Gardner's *The Parental Alienation Syndrome* and *The Differentiation Between Fabricated and Genuine Child Sex Abuse*.[6]

When there is clear evidence of a serious PAS during evaluation, it is our contention that this should be pointed out to the parents in a nonjudgmental, supportive manner. In cases where the "preferred" parent gains insight and has genuine understanding for the child's need to have a healthy relationship with both parents, corrective measures do not have to be as drastic as when the "preferred" parent continues to actively and obsessively program the child with hatred of the other parent. In cases where one parent is fanatical in their animosity, Gardner[6] recommends immediate placement of the child or children with the "hated" parent. This move is essential in attempting to save the precarious relationship between the child and "hated" parent. Since the "preferred" parent shows little or no insight into the current pathological process, the child in all likelihood would continue to be deluged with the denigration of the other parent should it remain in the "preferred" parent's home. Even therapy would not work in these cases if the child continues to reside with the vindictive parent. Further recommended by Gardner is that the "preferred" parent not be allowed direct access to the child for some period of time to allow the child an opportunity to reestablish bonds with the "hated" parent without subjecting the child to the loyalty conflicts inherent in the "preferred" parent's home. From one to a few months of no direct contact as well as treatment for the parents may suffice to overturn the pathological process. Indirect contact such as telephone calls to the "preferred" parent may be allowed if monitored. Following this period which should be under continual assessment by a competent mental health professional, a gradual return to more normal visitation patterns is recommended. These visitations should begin by being monitored as there is always the danger of a return to the pathological processes of PAS. Monitoring differs from supervised visits in that the professional monitoring is not necessarily physically present during the visits. Mental health professionals involved should meet together to gauge progress and make recommendations.

For parents who show insight into their pathological process, less extreme measures may be implemented. Depending upon the assessment, often individual, couple and/or family counseling may be enough to reverse the pathology. In spite of their previous negative programming, parents who are genuinely interested in the welfare of their children should voluntarily be willing to accept counseling. If parents do not accept the recommendations of the professional then perhaps the parents have been misdiagnosed and belong in a more pathological category.

In such cases it is usually preferable for the "hated" parent to have custody unless the basic Major and Minor Criteria strongly dictate otherwise. When there is significant PAS present it behoves the Team or expert to assess closely the bond between child and "preferred" parent. There is certainly always a strong bond between the two; however, the question is, is it a healthy bond? In our experience we have seen some strong, yet frighteningly unhealthy bonds between some parents and their children. Most noteworthy of these unhealthy bonds are when the child suffers from the aforementioned reverse symbiosis. In other words the child lives in order to take care of needs and feelings of the parent. Such children tend to lose themselves and their own individuality and have difficulty forming independent, healthy relationships as they develop.

In keeping within the spirit and ethics of the Team approach, any recommendations are to be made to the parents in order to decide for themselves. Clearly in situations when there is a highly pathological "brainwashing" parent there is almost no chance of succeeding without some form of court assistance. We would recommend strongly to judges and those attorneys who serve as guardian-ad-litem that should such a diagnosis be presented to them that they act swiftly. There is not that much time before the symptoms of PAS become so ingrained in a child that the child develops a personality-disordered type character which is quite resistant to change. We have witnessed at least one case where immediate placement to the father was recommended and the judge did not heed the recommendation. Currently this child is living with neither the father or mother and, in our opinion, has suffered nearly irreparable psychological damage. To date, this custody trial is about 2½ years old with no end in sight. Over a dozen experts have been involved due to the judge's uncertainty. While the judge clearly has compassionate motives for his indecision, the inclusion of a myriad of professionals in this case is a good example of "the cure being worse than the disease."

Sex and Other Abuse Charges in Custody Litigation

Another escalating phenomenon in child custody disputes is the incidence of child physical and especially sexual abuse allegations. For much the same reasons as in the development of PAS, parents are increasingly taking advantage of the current fervor regarding child sexual abuse. In fact, in more than half of the cases in which we have been involved where PAS was a significant factor, sex-abuse allegations have also been made. Many children's advocates contend that if a child makes an allegation of sex abuse it is invariably true. Prior to the early 1980s we would agree that this "truism" was probably accurate, especially in allegations not made in the context of a custody dispute. However, since the early 1980s a dramatic increase in the use of sexual abuse allegations within custody disputes has arisen. Again, we have Gardner[6] to thank for his detailed analysis of this phenomenon and measures to taken when confronted with abuse allegations.

Prior to the 1980s the general belief among professional advocates of "children never lie" was that children were not exposed to the kind of detailed sexual information which children who claimed to be abused were presenting to them. However, since that time children have been inundated with detailed sexual information from a myriad of sources including parents, sex education programs, sex abuse prevention programs, more sexually sophisticated peers, and television programs (both educational and dramatic). While some professionals do not as yet recognize the significance of this media exposure as leading to fabricated sexual abuse allegations, we certainly do, especially within the context of custody disputes. As Gardner[6] points out, "What more effective way could there be to get quick action by the courts than to allege a parent was molesting a child?"

Clearly, if a Team or other professional is to be thorough and objective in contemporary custody evaluations and investigations they must familiarize themselves with the current literature on sex abuse. At least one third of our caseload of custody evaluations involve child physical or sexual abuse allegations.

An allegation of suspected physical or sexual abuse of children by a custodial or noncustodial parent is obviously extremely serious, particularly if the allegation is true. But it also warrants a thorough, conscientious investigation due to the fact that if one parent knowingly makes a serious abuse allegation involving the other parent without factual basis to form reasonable suspicion, then the results can be devastating for the alleged child victim as well as for the perpetrator. There are instances in which serious allegations have been made up by a parent, or a child has been encouraged to give false information to professionals who are mandated by law to report suspected child abuse or neglect. This is done with hope that the end result will be that the parent making the allegation will be awarded permanent legal custody of the child or children involved in the contested custody litigation. An allegation of physical and/or sexual abuse can be the result of any of the following possibilities: (1) a parent may have genuine concern regarding the possibility that a son or daughter may have been abused as the result of comments made by the child and/or observations of unexplained injuries to the child or injuries in which the alleged perpetrator's explanation for the child's injury is inconsistent with the nature of the injury (for example, an explanation that a child was scraped while playing ball but there are observable injuries resembling numerous cigarette burns on the child's arms, legs and back); (2) a parent may be so determined to obtain legal custody of the children that the parent will make up allegations involving the other parent or will encourage the child to make suggestive comments to others. Based on the comments a child makes, a professional may conclude that there is basis to suspect that the child has been abused by one of the parents; or (3) a child may have a strong preference for the mother and due to a concern that the father may be granted custody, may decide to allege that he or she was physically or sexually abused by the father. The child in this instance probably does not realize the seriousness of such allegations or the implication that a serious abuse investigation will in all likelihood begin soon after the allegation is brought to the attention of any professional who is mandated to report suspected neglect or abuse of children. A further complication is the fact that it is often extremely difficult to determine if the abuse actually occurred. In the majority of alleged sexual abuse cases, it is typical to have the child's version of the alleged abuse countered by the alleged perpetrator's denial of the truth of the allegation. In most sexual abuse cases as well as in many cases of physical abuse of children, there are no witnesses that could be interviewed in order to help determine the truth of the allegation. Many types of sexual abuse can occur without any medical evidence being possible. Many injuries to children are not the result of physical abuse but are injuries resulting from accidents. If a child is not old enough to be a credible witness, it becomes even more difficult to determine the real cause of injuries or symptomology to children.

If there is substantial evidence that abuse has occurred (e.g., confession, court findings, etc.), it is important to determine the extent of the abuse, the frequency of abusive incidents, the age of the child who has been abused, the contributing factors that helped lead to the abuse taking place, and the real effects upon the child of the abuse. Within the context of custody and visitation recommendations it is also important to consider the perpetrator's attitude toward the abuse, the perpetrating parent's willingness to correct the conditions that are the basis for the abuse, and the motivation of the parent to learn healthy ways to deal with the underlying feelings and needs causitive of the abusive behavior. The abuse incident should also be viewed in the context of all other factors relating to the perpetrator's situation as well as the factors relating to the other parent's situation. For example, one parent may physically abuse a child on one occasion resulting in a small bruise on the child's buttock area. Investigation of that same parent reveals a loving parent who is quite capable of assuming parental responsibilities for the child, the parent who has been the one who has assumed responsibility for the majority of child care tasks since the child's birth, and a parent who has no past history of abusive or neglectful behavior or of exhibiting any emotional problems. The nonabusive parent may be an alcoholic and/or drug addict with poor prognosis for recovering from the addiction. If the parent's drug or alcohol addiction interferes significantly with his or her parenting abilities (both quantity of time the parent spends with the child in addition to the quality of parenting), then the abusive parent in this instance may be the better alternative when considering the best long-range plan for the child.

Abuse allegations should always be taken seriously within the context of custody evaluations and investigations. It is as important to determine if one of the parents is consciously or unconsciously attempting to manipulate the custody determination though nonfactual allegations as it is to determine that the abuse is probably bonafide. In some cases even the child denies the allegations, but the accuser-parent persists in attempting to convince authorities and the child that the allegations are true.

It cannot be stressed enough that any abuse or neglect allegations must be viewed within the context of the validity of the allegation as well as other factors involved in the child's situation in each litigant's home. It is not just one fact or nebulous accusation that determines the best interests of a child or family. It is a combination of attitudes and behaviors of parents. It is important for custody evaluators and investigators to keep a broad perspective when confronted with actual, fabricated, or suspected abuse and neglect charges. It is easy for even well-intentioned evaluators to get caught up in what is urgent, losing perspective of what is important.

Gardner[6] has developed what is probably the first objective measure in the field of differentiating bona fide from fabricated sexual abuse allegations. When such charges are a part of the custody evaluation, it is necessary for contemporary professionals to be familiar with this scale (The Sex Abuse Legitimacy Scale). In some cases we handle, the sex or physical abuse charges have already been thoroughly investigated and determinations have already been made. Often, we have cases in which allegations have been founded or unfounded by the Department of Children and Family Services. In some founded cases, the courts have taken no action due to the more scrutinous criteria for evidence required by the courts than is the case for founded reports by children's service agencies. In this type of case, the team or professional should undertake a further investigation of the charges using Gardner's *Sex Abuse Legitimacy Scale* mentioned above. Even in unfounded cases, the matter of sex abuse charges should not be dropped as there is much valuable information to be learned. Remember, it is as crucial to assess whether charges are likely or highly likely to be fabricated as it is to ascertain if the charges are likely or highly likely to be true. The fact that a parent accuser continues to righteously insist that abuse took place when all evidence dictates otherwise is just as crucial to the Team's custody analysis as is the forthright denial of the alleged perpetrator parent when there is ample evidence to suspect abuse.

One of the main advantages of independent, objective examination by a Team or evaluator is that the Team is not constricted by courtroom rules. Because of this we can get all parties together in the same room speaking for themselves, not speaking through an attorney. When physical or sexual abuse is at issue the Team or evaluator has a decided advantage in that the alleged perpetrator, the alleged victim, and the accuser can be interviewed not only separately, but jointly. Some may argue that a joint meeting of the alleged victim and perpetrator parent is too traumatic for the victim. While this may be true in some cases, it is our experience that this is generally not true, especially when the allegations are likely fabricated. Children are much more resilient than we often give them credit for. Also, even if the charges are true, the fact remains that the perpetrator is a parent and will undoubtedly maintain or reestablish a relationship with the victim. Often this confrontation serves as "breaking the ice" for future therapeutic efforts to heal that relationship even if the accusations are true. The tremendous advantage of such a meeting in disputed sex and physical abuse cases normally far outweighs its potential disadvantages. An astute evaluator can usually gain valuable information not only as to the credibility of the charges in question, but also into the character and sensitivity of the alleged perpetrator parent as well as the accuser parent.

Gardner's *Sex Abuse Legitimacy Scale* contains a simple yes/no questionnaire for the evaluator to fill out. He has divided criteria for determination of sex abuse into three categories: (1) very valuable, (2) moderately valuable, and (3) low but potentially higher value. He utilizes these three categories for each of the three parties involved: (1) alleged perpetrator, (2) alleged victim, and (3) the accuser. A composite score of each of the three parties involved is tabulated and rated in one of three categories: (1) sex abuse allegation is extremely likely to have been fabricated, (2) results are inconclusive, and (3) sex abuse allegation is strongly suggestive of bona fide sex abuse. Utilizing this scale along with other information, especially medical data when available, is extremely valuable when evaluating for custody and visitation recommendations.

As a final note on this topic, we wish to acknowledge the extreme sensitivity and potentially volatile nature of such investigations, especially when done in connection with a custody dispute. Undoubtedly there are errors made on both sides in terms of guilt or innocence. In our experience we have seen the system use very poor and inappropriate methods in assessing sex abuse. For example, not interviewing the alleged perpetrator prior to findings, utilizing children's counselors as objective evaluators, and generally presuming the guilt of alleged perpetrators until proven innocent. What is important in this regard is not that we make mistakes, but that we learn from them and create a more objective, thorough and humane system of evaluating this explosive issue. As mental health professionals we must aid each other in order to assist the children and families we serve. There appears to be a strong trend for children's service professionals to serve as attorneys, judges and police in these matters. This is not our role, and in our opinion, such assumed roles are a part of the problem in the field of abuse investigation, not a part of the solution. As mental health professionals we are neither trained nor qualified to assume such roles. Our commitment calls for compassionate and objective evaluation and treatment of our clients. Some may call this stance idealistic. I prefer to call it realistic as there is nothing more idealistic than to think we can create a better world through fear, intimidation, and aggression.

Chapter IX

AIMING FOR THE FUTURE

Ending Adversarial Litigation in Custody Disputes

Throughout history society's attitude regarding placement of children following divorce has changed. During the Roman Empire, when divorce was fairly rampant, fathers were the automatic custodians of children. This trend lasted until approximately the mid-nineteenth century when the "tender years presumption" began to become popular. This presumption asserted that during the formative years of a child the mother was biologically and psychologically superior to the father as a parent. In the early development of the "tender years presumption," once the children attained the age of three or four they were once again turned over to fathers. Due primarily to the women's liberation movement and to the establishment of child labor laws in the early 1900s, the attitudes of society and the courts began to change. Children were no longer an economic asset and women were gaining power through access to education and other forms of training previously closed to them. The change which took place in the 1920s would last until the 1970s. States changed their laws so that only parenting factors, not related to the sex of a parent, were relevant in determining custody. Nevertheless, these "sex-blind" laws were generally administered in the favor of women. This trend lasted until the 1970s when "male consciousness" was being raised and such concepts as androgyny were becoming popular, especially among the educated. Such pressure on the legislatures and courts resulted in more true "sex-blind" decisions whereby fathers had a real chance for custody.

Since the early 1970s courts no longer have an easy and automatic task based upon societal norms. Now a detailed assessment of each parent's character, lifestyle, and financial assets had to be gathered by the court in order to even approximate a judicious decision. Currently the system once used only to determine guilt and innocence in criminal and civil matters is now being utilized to determine custody; namely, the adversarial system. The resources of the court are extremely limited in determining such factors as character, lifestyle, and motivation of the adversaries. Consequently, mental health experts are being called upon to assist the courts in these matters. Unfortunately, under the existing laws governing adversarial litigation, each side has not only a right to an attorney, but a right to a mental health expert as well. One can readily begin to smell the uncomely fragrance of a stew brewed by so many cooks.

As Gardner[1] has aptly pointed out, the outcome of such protracted litigation is a tremendous increase in custody related psychiatric disturbances in parents and children. We would like to believe that once custody has been awarded the related mental health disturbances would disappear. However, it is naive to believe such. The very nature of adversarial litigation brings out the worst in people. Often the scars of battle are felt long after the battle is fought and decided. While many generally healthy children do get over their psychological wounds once the decision is made, many do not. The prime example of this is children who suffer Parent Alienation Syndrome. Also, as those of us who do relationship therapy can attest, there are some things that can be said or done from which it is all but impossible to heal or to ever again trust. This is as true for parents as for children. Many mild to devastating ills occur as a result of adversarial custody litigation. It behooves all of us who either have knowledge of these ills or who have the authority to change the breeding ground for these ills, to work together to create a system that is, at once, more humane, less traumatic, more efficient, and more preventative.

A Pilot Project

Thanks to judiciary foresight in the 20th Judicial District in Southern Illinois a pilot project called *Children First** is in effect for parents who have children and are divorcing. *Children First* is a straightforward educational project geared to make parents aware of the psychological maladies that can result from typical custody disputes. When individuals in the district file for divorce they are instructed to call the *Children First* program. They are informed that no further action on their divorce will take place until they have completed the two one-hour course meetings.

---

*Currently the Children First program is scheduled to be implemented in the southern-most counties of Illinois as well. The credit for this innovative program goes to Dr. Dan Cuneo of the Chester Mental Health Center and to Dr. Gene Ringuette, a retired professor from the psychology department at Southern Illinois University.

The hour-long course meetings consist of groups of up to ten parents. Spouses are never in the same group. Taped vignettes of typical dysfunctional behavior by divorcing parents toward their children are shown. There are six vignettes in all and three per session are usually played. The tapes of the professionally made video vignettes include parents who make promises they don't keep, parents who use visitation to manipulate their spouse, and parents who fight in front of their children. Following each vignette the parents discuss the theme with the assistance of a trained mental health professional. If the parents have questions, the mental health counselor assists them with answers or other resources. The cost for the program is determined by a sliding scale from no cost to $75.00. About $20.00 is the average cost for the two-hour program. In addition to the video vignettes, various handouts are distributed which contain the general "do's and don'ts" of parenting children of divorce.

Alternative Models to Adversarial Litigation

While the *Children First* prevention program is a giant step in the right direction, it would be naive to assume that such programs would suffice to significantly reduce the psychological damage caused by adversarial litigation. What is needed is a major overhaul of the law and procedures governing custody disputes. More ideal would be a combination of such educational and preventative programs as *Children First* along with the extinction of the adversarial process. What would replace the adversarial process?

The majority of this book has been devoted to how to more humanely and efficiently perform child custody evaluations within the existing laws of most states governing custody litigation. We propose the legalization of the Family's Team approach or of another acceptable approach which empowers the parents, provides them with much needed assistance in coming to conclusions themselves, and, if all else fails, provides the parents with a decision which has been well worked out by appropriate professionals.

The Model

Our hypothetical model would provide court jurisdiction over Teams available to be appointed by the assigning judge whenever necessary to settle child custody and visitation disputes. The Team would consist of an evaluator, investigator, and an attorney for the family. Some of the larger courts already have psychologists and social workers employed. Where this is not the case, the court can have a list of qualified and trained psychologists from which to appoint evaluators. Social worker investigators can be obtained through the offices of the Department of Children and Family Services. Family attorneys can be appointed by the court in the same fashion as is currently used in assigning a guardian-ad-litem to a case.

The Team would have full legal authority to settle the matter of custody and visitation subject to review by the assigned judge who would ascertain that all applicable rights of the family were protected. The Team would utilize methodology from mediation, arbitration, family law, and the evaluative/investigative process described in this and other pertinent literature. Methods utilized by the Team would be dictated by the readiness of the litigants to mediate or arbitrate. Initially, a strong educational program including methods utilized by the *Children First* program as well as methods described in this book could be presented in an attempt to produce a more cooperative attitude among the parents leading to an early resolution of the custody dispute.

Ideally, the Team should not always consist of the same members. This can lead to stagnation and loss of creativity. A number of various interested and dedicated professionals should be trained and ready to serve as Team members. Once such a program is initiated, new candidates for the Team can obtain on-the-job training by exposure as assistant Team members. The use of videotape can further assist in the training of Team members as well as help improve Team skills.

The feedback from attorneys concerning legalizing the Team approach has produced three major areas of concern. First of all there is some concern that judges would be reluctant to give up their decision making role. Secondly, attorneys may resist such legislation because it may reduce their income from divorce cases. Thirdly, the costs of running such a program would be prohibitive and there are no federal, state, or local funds available to pay for private evaluators and Family's attorneys.

We will address each of these three concerns separately:

1. While there are undoubtedly judges who are so psychologically threatened that they cannot envision anyone but themselves making just decisions, such judges are extremely rare in our experience. Given the tremendous increase in judicial use of expert witnesses in custody cases, most judges welcome competent, objective, and professional insight into these difficult decisions. The relevant issues concerning custody, such as

personality, parenting ability, credibility, bonding, motivation, etc., are all the domains of the mental health expert and competent judges welcome the expert's testimony. Our prediction is that most judges would be greatly relieved to have such complex and confounding decisions in more appropriate hands.

2. It is true that attorneys will suffer some financial loss by not representing clients fully in the custody aspect of divorce. Attorneys will, however, retain their position of representing clients in all other aspects of divorce. Many attorneys have informed me that the custody aspect of divorce cases is not only their least favorite task, but also the most personally painful. Many, in fact, have discontinued any work on the custody aspect of divorce altogether. Attorneys are human like the rest of us, and they are not immune to the pain and humiliation done to children and families through custody litigation. Competent attorneys do their utmost to represent their clients, but this does not mean that they always believe in their clients or even like them. They, too, must go home after work each day and are subject to as much guilt and remorse as anyone when they advocate causes they know are hurtful to children. Attorneys were once vehemently opposed to the practice of divorce mediation/arbitration at the beginning of its popularity about a decade ago. Now many endorse this process of resolving divorce via mediation/arbitration. I suspect that they soon realized not only the benefits of this humane process, but also that there was still plenty of work to go around if one was competent enough.

3. Probably the greatest obstacle to more enlightened divorce and custody litigation is the issue of funding. No new legislation should be implemented, however justified, without a sound financial plan to support such legislation. Witness the enlightened legislation regarding the right of special education students in the United States in 1974. Public Law 94-142 was going to provide every special education student with whatever he or she needed in order to gain a proper education. This promising legislation has since turned into an administrative nightmare for most districts. The promising legislation was passed, but there was no commensurate funding. School districts simply did not have the finances for such demands as came to them. Consequently the courts were inundated with lawsuits against school districts, which, for the most part, were operating in the "red" anyway. This legislation has been a financial nightmare for countless school districts and parents of children with special needs.

On the surface the proposed Family's Team approach to resolving custody would appear to be very costly. Rather than a judge who is salaried, we are proposing a team of three professionals who have to be paid. It is our contention that with some creative thought and planning this objection can be overcome. Following are some possible solutions to this very real dilemma:

1. Adversarial attorneys spend a disproportionate amount of time just on the custody aspect of divorce. As mentioned in a previous chapter, the scope of potential testimony regarding custody ranges from the birth of each litigant to the time when all children involved become legal adults. Any competent family law attorney will use whatever she or he judges to be effective for their clients within their range. Typical custody court proceedings involve dozens of collateral witnesses and even a handful of experts who analyze the past and predict the future. Even private detectives are not unheard of and will investigate litigants' past behavior back into grade school. In most criminal proceedings only testimony is allowed which is clearly relevant to a specific time, place, and behavior. The scope and range of testimony is much more restricted and manageable than testimony in custody proceedings. The money spent on such proceedings comes out of the client's pocket. Under our proposal, judges would be mandated to appoint any custody dispute to the Team. Judges would continue to have the authority to delegate payment by the clients in the same manner as they do now when they order a psychological evaluation of all parties. Thus, the money which once went to attorneys for their time-consuming effort concerning custody could be placed in a fund administered by the court to pay for the Team's services. It is not out of line with reality that between attorneys and private experts most litigants spend over $4000 each just on the custody aspect of divorce. As we hope to make clear, this sum is more than adequate to meet the Team's financial needs. Attorneys would need to adjust their billing procedures accordingly when custody is involved. An attorney's retainer or bill would not include any monies for custody-related issues.

2. Under our proposal, the Team's initial function would be to educate and inform the parents, expanding upon the procedures found in the *Children First* program and this book. Should parents decide to mediate and/or arbitrate at this early point in the proceedings, costs could be held to a minimum. The education of the parents could include description of the full-fledged investigation and evaluation, the costs, and a description of the Major and Minor Criteria. Following the educational component and the procedural explanation of the Team's task,

many parents would likely feel that it would be best to settle the matter of custody themselves. Under the present adversarial system parents are often not directly questioned and confronted because no one has given them the in-depth information concerning the rigors and objectivity of the evaluation and investigation. Consequently, parents turn over the decision-making power to a judge who often has to decide who is more believable without the sound and credible evidence that can only be obtained by the procedures and interviewing techniques described in this or similar texts. Thus, the educational component, including the interviewing technique of direct questioning of the parents together without an attorney speaking for them will doubtlessly result in swifter, more efficient, less costly (to the parents), and more humane resolution of the custody dispute. As mentioned earlier I have been to court on only about three occasions in the past five years as a result of the methods described in this book.

3. The Team's investigator could be supplied from a pool of trained professionals within a Department of Children and Family Services. This would save considerable expense at the same time as providing consistent professional expertise. This service should be a clear mandate of state children's agencies as both children and families are at considerable risk in custody battles.

4. The Family's attorney has minimal involvement in the Team's investigation and evaluation. She or he needs to be present at some meetings and review the results in light of family law. This service can be ordered pro bona and/or the family can be assessed a fee by the judge. This is not much different from current law and procedures.

5. If legislated appropriately, the major costs would be the fee of the independent evaluator whenever the court does not have a professional mental health expert as part of its salaried staff. Independent evaluations will generally cost between $500 and $2500 depending upon the complexities of the case (e.g., physical or sexual abuse allegations, drug or alcohol addictions, psychiatric history, etc.) and the willingness of the parties to arbitrate and/or mediate. As mentioned, the costs for the evaluator can be readily obtained by charging the parties themselves. Funds earmarked for attorneys to fight for custody are much more judiciously spent on a nonadversarial, problem solving method which helps alleviate family pathology. Much destructive and even criminal behavior is fostered along in the family law courtroom.

For indigent clients a fund can be established with revenues collected from past evaluations. For example, the court can generally bill $100 to $150 per hour for Family's Team work. If only an independent evaluator needs to be paid between $50 and $75 per hour and a Family's attorney $100 to $200 for a few hours work, then the excess can be channeled into a fund for use with those who cannot pay. Also, a sliding scale could be used and evaluators can contribute some of their time as a public service. There are undoubtedly many creative solutions to the funding problem once the process reaches legislative involvement. What is critical is to be ready once legislation is passed. We do not want to make the same error that was made with special education legislation.

Concluding Comments

One of the major purposes of this book has been to help serve as a catalyst for change in the way states handle custody litigation. By utilizing the ethics and methods in this book it has been the exception, not the rule, that families have had to go to court armed with their lies, embellishments, and righteousness. We would like to see all custody settled more humanely, more efficiently and with less trauma to families. Custody litigation is not only increasing, but is becoming more complex, emotionally violent, and more emotionally and financially costly. Litigants and bright attorneys are utilizing the contemporary federal trend toward human rights as a license to intimidate and accost other human beings using the well-being of children as justification. The basic "right" to charge anyone with sex abuse and have it investigated any number of times seems to me to give "license" to harass and ruin another person. The basic right to a hearing concerning the future welfare of children seems to give "license" for many to emotionally torture, lie, physically abuse and attempt to annihilate the self-esteem of one of their own children's parents. Clearly none of this is virtuous. Whenever the balance between the ethics of rights and the ethics of virtue are out of balance in this manner, it creates a litigious, paranoid and narcissistic culture. This is the state of affairs in contemporary America. Our basic rights in America were intended to produce equality and freedom, not to give license to the stronger or cleverer to pursue his or her unvirtuous ends. Should we succeed in changing how custody is decided, we will have taken a step in reestablishing this balance between the ethics of rights and the ethics of virtue. Gardner[1] opened his book with a quote from a petition for a Writ of Certiorari submitted to the Supreme Court of the United States by Cleveland attorney Sanford J. Berger on behalf of a divorced client's request for protection from cruel and unusual punishment (associated with penalties suffered in divorce litigation). We wish to end with this same quote:

> "In all that is decent . . . in all that is just, the framers of our Constitution could never have intended that the "enjoyment of life" meant that if divorce came, it was to be attended by throwing the two unfortunates and their children into a judicial arena, with lawyers as their seconds, and have them tear and verbally slash at each other in a trial by emotional conflict that may go on in perpetuity. We have been humane enough to outlaw cockfights, dogfights, and bullfights; and yet, we do nothing about the barbarism of divorce fighting, and trying to find ways to end it. We concern ourselves with cruelty to animals, and rightfully so, but we are unconcerned about the forced and intentionally perpetrated cruelty inflicted upon the emotionally distressed involved in divorce. We abhor police beating confessions out of alleged criminals, and yet we cheer and encourage lawyers to emotionally beat up and abuse two innocent people and their children, because their marriage has floundered. Somewhere along the line, our sense of values, decency, humanism, and justice went off the track."

APPENDICES

1. Criteria Worksheet
2. Letter of Conditions and Procedures
3. Parental Intake Form
4. Child Care Responsibilities
5. True-False Questionnaires for Litigants
6. Questionnaire for Litigants
7. Combination Completion/True-False Form for Litigants
8. Completion Form for Litigants (1)
9. Completion Form for Litigants (2)
10. Completion Form for Litigants (3)
11. Completion Form for Litigants (4)
12. Form for Litigants
13. Completion Form for Children (1)
14. Completion Form for Children (2)
15. Completion Form for Children (3)
16. Completion Form for Children (4)
17. True-False Questionnaire for Children
18. Additional Questions to Utilize in Interviewing Children
19. Additional Questions for Litigants in Custody Case
20. Statement of Understanding Regarding Confidentiality
21. Form Letter to Send to School if School Age Children
22. School Report Form To Be Utilized in Custody Investigations
23. Law Enforcement Form
24. Collateral Form
25. Verification of Employment Form
26. Sample, Nonbinding, Parental Agreement
27. Sample Investigative Custody Report

1. CRITERIA WORKSHEET

Name of Parent:

Case Number:

Children Involved and Ages:

MAJOR CRITERIA:

1. *Psychological Parenting:* Give opinion as to this parent's status and ability to be a psychological parent:

2. *Continuity of Relationship:* List all the dates the litigant has had each separate child in their care (exclude normal visitation) since the family unit has broken up.

3. *Emotional Stability:* Give an opinion as to this parent's emotional stability, especially as it relates to the children. Be prepared to support your opinion with specific data and testing.

4. *Continuity of Sibling Relationship:* Document and support any opinion that deviates from the norm of not separating siblings.

5. *Parent Flexibility:* Give an opinion of this parent's ability to be a low or high conflict parent as it relates to his/her contact with the other parent regarding the children. Be prepared to support opinion with specific data.

6. *Physical Health:* Specify this litigant's physical ability to handle child-rearing. List any significant illnesses or physical disabilities.

MINOR CRITERIA:

1. *Parent's Moral Character:* List only *documented* evidence of this litigant's immoral characteristics. Any immoral characteristics must be based upon contemporary social standards and the law. Lying, cheating, abandonment of children, illegal occupations, spouse or child abuse, etc. are characteristics which could be listed.

2. *Parent's Financial, Material, Cultural Assets:* List and document the assets applicable to this litigant.

3. *Favoring a Two-Parent Home:* Describe current marital status or live-in paramour arrangements of this litigant.

4. *Wishes of the Children:* Describe the explicit or implied wishes of the children for custody. Are the wishes genuine or the result of an unhealthy symbiosis or Parent Alienation Syndrome?

5. *Favoring Child's Access to Extended Family:* List the extended family members available to the children of the litigant. Are these relationships already developed? What is the current quality of these relationships?

Synopsis of Findings: Place a "P" by each number corresponding to each of the Major and Minor Criterion if this litigant is the preferred parent in corresponding category.

Major Criteria:

1.   4.

2.   5.

3.   6.

Minor Criteria:

1.   4.

2.   5.

3.

Is this the parent or guardian who has provided most of the day-to-day parenting during children's formative years (0–5)?

Yes _____ No _____

Comments?

2. LETTER OF CONDITIONS AND PROCEDURES

Custody Evaluations

My involvement in custody evaluations is dependent on the following conditions:

(1) That both parties and their attorneys agree to me being appointed to evaluate the entire family. In my years of custody work I have seen incredible harm come to children and parents through the legal adversarial process itself and compounded further by the use not only of adversarial attorneys, but also of adversarial psychologists.

(2) That both contesting parties understand and accept that I will base my findings and recommendations *solely* on what I believe is in the best interests of the children regardless of the source of my fee.

(3) That both parents understand that I will strongly recommend to all attorneys and parents involved to settle the matter of custody outside of the legal adversarial system based upon mediation and/or arbitration. Again, the reason for this is that the adversarial system was not meant for domestic cases for child custody and *always* causes psychological damage to both children and their parents.

(4) That a retainer fee of $ _____ be paid to me in advance. The usual method is for the parties to split this fee; however, whatever agreements are made by the parties and their attorneys is acceptable. My fees are $70 per hour and $100 per hour in court.

(5) That both parties agree to release to me all information which I desire pertinent to the evaluation (e.g., past police or mental health records).

The usual procedure for custody evaluations is:

(1) Upon acceptance of my conditions I will set up appointments with all relevant parties. A Parental Intake Form will be sent to each party to have filled out prior to the first meeting.

(2) Prior to any formal interviews the parents come to the office at their convenience to fill out several forms and questionnaires and to take the Minnesota Multiphasic Personality Inventory (MMPI). This procedure usually will take three to four hours. The parents pay their retainer fee at this time.

(3) When all forms, questionnaires, and testing is completed, I meet with both parents together, with each parent separately, with each child separately, and with each parent and child separately. Additional interviews will be arranged as needed.

(4) Upon completion of examination (which may include several meetings) I will go over my results and contact any other relevant parties in order to verify my data. This process can take one to four weeks.

(5) If the parents have not yet come to an agreement as to custody and visitation through mediation/arbitration, the parents will be invited to a meeting which may include the parents, any guardian-ad-litem, any court-appointed investigator, and me. I will go over the conclusions and recommendations with the parents. After correcting any incorrect facts or opinions I will encourage the parents to settle the custody matter out of court using the data presented them as a guideline. Should the

parents decide to come to an agreement, they will be instructed that their agreement will not be binding until they have consulted with their attorneys and have signed a valid legal document.

(6) Should the parents not agree to an out-of-court settlement, they will be given a copy of the final Criteria Worksheet to present to their attorneys. This will contain my opinion on each of the Major and Minor Criteria for custody which I utilize. A formally written report reflective of the conclusions and recommendations will be sent to the court and to both attorneys.

3. PARENTAL INTAKE FORM

FORM TO BE COMPLETED BY PERSONS INVOLVED IN CHILD CUSTODY LITIGATION

(Relevant Information Related to a Child Custody Proceeding)

Names and birthdates of children involved in current custody proceedings:

Court Number and County of Jurisdiction:

Name of person wanting custody of above-named child or children:

Address:

Telephone number:

Directions to home:

Legal name (wife's maiden):

Name of family physician:

Present Situation—State your reason for wanting custody of above child or children: (use additional sheets if necessary):

Family Composition—List names, birthdates, and birthplaces of all persons currently residing in your home—include relationship of each person to you:

Current Living Arrangements: Please list number of bedrooms and list other rooms in home:

Length of time at above address:

Are you currently renting or do you own your home:

Education: List highest grade completed for each adult member of household; list grade in school, name of school and school address for each school age child:

Health: List current state of health of each person in the household. If any medical problems, please specify type of problem including any medications taken:

Employment: If employed, list employer's name, address, present occupation and length of time on present job:

If not presently employed, please list previous employment:

Income: List amount of current gross monthly income and source of income:

Marital History: List current marital status, list dates of all marriages, including dates of divorces, deaths or separation:

Interests and Activities: List current interests and activities:

List religious preference, if any: List name and address of church attended on a regular basis:

List any involvement with the police of any member in household, including any court convictions or charges:

Describe each child involved in current custody litigation:

List advantages and disadvantages to the child or children if you were to obtain legal custody:

List discipline methods utilized by you:

List your perception of the most important needs of children:

What are your main strengths as a parent or parent substitute:

What do you consider to be your main weaknesses as a parent or parent substitute:

List your plans for child care in the event you obtain legal custody of the child or children involved:

Please list names, addresses and phone numbers of persons you would like worker to contact who would have relevant information in regard to custody matter:

(Signature of Person Completing Form)

(Date Completed)

4. CHILD CARE RESPONSIBILITIES

Listed below are typical child care responsibilities experienced by parents or parent substitutes. Please be sure to place the correct number (utilizing your choices below listed 1 through 4) beside each task that applies to your situation. Please choose the answer that most closely relates to each task.

Please complete the form as it relates to your situation from the time your child or children were first born to the time you and your spouse or ex-spouse's most recent separation or divorce (or until the initiation of the current custody proceedings). Please indicate all child care tasks that not only are more recently applicable, but those that were applicable from the time of your child's birth up to the present time.

1. Usually performed by me.
2. Usually performed by my spouse or ex-spouse.
3. Usually performed by both my spouse or ex-spouse and me.
4. Usually performed by another person; if this is the most correct answer, please list name of person who usually performs the task as well as the person's relationship to the child or children after the number.

CHILD CARE TASK OR ACTIVITY

1. Waking child up each morning.
2. Seeing that child eats breakfast.
3. Dressing child.
4. Selecting child's clothes.
5. Seeing that child goes to school.
6. Preparing meals for child.
7. Taking the child to doctor's appointments.
8. Taking the child to dentist appointments.
9. Enrolling child in school.
10. Talking with school staff in regard to child's progress.
11. Attend school functions such as open house.
12. Taking care of child during child's illness.
13. Bathes child.
14. Changing diapers.
15. Washing child's hair.
16. Getting child ready for bed.
17. Taking child for haircuts.
18. Taking child's temperature during illness.
19. Taking child to specialist if indicated.
20. Potty training.
21. Purchases clothes for child.
22. Helps child with school work.
23. Reading to child.
24. Talking to child about daily events.

25. Playing with child.
26. Seeing that child gets to bed at a designated time.
27. Selects gifts for child for holidays such as Christmas or birthdays.
28. Spending time teaching values to child.
29. Answering child's questions.
30. Discussing with child concerns a child expresses.
31. Supervising child.
32. Taking child to day care and/or school program.
33. Seeing that child practices good personal hygiene.
34. Provides child with educational opportunities.
35. Spends time in recreational activities with child.
36. Disciplines child when needed.
37. Assumes responsibility for the majority of child care tasks.

Appendices

5. TRUE-FALSE QUESTIONS FOR LITIGANTS

Please answer the following true or false questions. Circle a T for true or an F for false after each statement based on your beliefs and values.

T F 1. If my spouse or ex-spouse did not have so many faults, our marriage would have been successful.

T F 2. If a child cannot live with both parents, it is important that they take sides and express their preference to both parents so that it is clear where the child's loyalties lie.

T F 3. If your child lives with you for several years and you have legal custody and later on your child expresses a desire to live with the noncustodial parent, the child's wish should not be given serious consideration.

T F 4. Children should appreciate the fact that if it was not for them, I would not be in this mess now.

T F 5. Children should not express their ideas or opinions on important issues concerning them.

T F 6. I find it difficult to say anything positive about my spouse or ex-spouse.

T F 7. I would be happier if my spouse or ex-spouse would be denied any visitation rights.

T F 8. I try to get detailed information about my spouse or ex-spouse from my child after each visit my child has with my spouse or ex-spouse.

T F 9. If my child refused to visit my spouse or ex-spouse, I would permit my child to not visit even if I did not know any legitimate reason for my child's refusing to visit.

T F 10. If my child is old enough to get an allowance, I would expect him or her to pay for his own telephone calls to my spouse or ex-spouse.

T F 11. I believe it would be wise for people to wait longer before having responsibilities of raising children.

T F 12. I was sexually abused when I was a child.

T F 13. I was physically abused when I was a child.

T F 14. I find it difficult to express affection to my child.

T F 15. If I lost custody in court, I would actually be relieved.

T F 16. Children have a responsibility to meet the needs of their parents.

T F 17. I am happier when my child does not enjoy being with my spouse or ex-spouse.

6. QUESTIONNAIRE FOR LITIGANTS

Please circle any opportunity or experience listed below (if any) that you would object to your son or daughter experiencing. *Keep in mind that it is assumed that each experience would be at a time that was age appropriate for your son or daughter to participate in each activity, your son or daughter is not opposed to the opportunity, and your son or daughter would not be in any danger.*

1. Opportunity to play with and get to know children of other races or cultures.
2. Opportunity to play with and get to know children of other socioeconomic backgrounds.
3. Opportunity to associate with children who have physical problems (such as epilepsy or multiple sclerosis).
4. Opportunity to visit museums.
5. Learn a foreign language.
6. If attends college, being able to have a roomate who is a different race than your son or daughter.
7. Eat foods from other cultures or countries.
8. Attend (as a visitor) a church service that is a different denomination than you attend or are the most familiar with.
9. An opportunity to talk to an inmate incarcerated at one of the prisons in this vicinity.
10. An opportunity to travel to other countries.
11. A chance to do volunteer work in a ghetto.
12. A chance to do work with alcoholics.
13. An opportunity to do work with drug addicts.
14. An opportunity to do volunteer work in a mental hospital.
15. An opportunity to work with juvenile delinquents.
16. A chance to attend a lecture given by a person who was previously a prostitute but now tries to help teenagers *not* be involved in illegal activities.
17. An opportunity to become friends with a foreign exchange student from another country.

7. COMBINATION COMPLETION TRUE-FALSE FORM FOR LITIGANTS

1. Three of my best friends are _____.
2. In selecting friends, I try to select friends with the following qualities: _____.
3. My child prefers to live with _____.
4. If I had to select one factor in my spouse's or ex-spouse's lifestyle that would concern me the most, it would be _____.
5. Recording telephone conversations of my child's conversations with my spouse or ex-spouse _____.
6. If my child decided to quit school when 15½ or 16 years old, I would _____.
7. If my child wants to drink alcoholic beverages or use marijuana while a teenager, I would _____.

T F 1. I permit my child to have friends visit in our home.
T F 2. I have concerns about my spouse or ex-spouse's friends.
T F 3. My spouse's or ex-spouse's current lifestyle adversely affects our child.
T F 4. I would allow smoking and/or drinking alcoholic beverages in front of my child.
T F 5. I would or have permitted persons of the opposite sex as myself to stay all night in my home.
T F 6. It is better to leave some subjects such as sex or AIDS as subjects that should not be discussed with children.
T F 7. I have or would tape record conversations of my child regarding custody issues if it would help my court case.

8. COMPLETION FORM FOR LITIGANTS (1)

Please complete each sentence with the first ideas that come to your mind.

1. An example of the most educational activity or opportunity I personally provided for my child was _____.
2. One of the most nutritional meals a child could have would include _____.
3. My spouse's or ex-spouse's parental strengths include _____.
4. My spouse's or ex-spouse's parental weaknesses include _____.
5. An educational TV program beneficial for children to watch would be ____.
6. If I hear persons relating negative information or criticisms about my ex-spouse or spouse in front of my child, it would be best to _____.
7. One of the most difficult experiences related to divorce would include ____.
8. If my child wanted me to attend a program he or she would be participating in the same night I planned to attend a game or concert, I would probably ____.
9. If my child wants to choose an occupation different from what I would prefer would be chosen, it would be best to _____.
10. If I only had a week left to live, I would _____.
11. If I was physically incapable of taking care of my child or children, it would be best to _____.
12. I would like to be remembered as _____.
13. If I have plane tickets to leave for vacation and the day before I am to leave my child is hospitalized for the first time, I would _____.
14. If I won $10,000.00, I would _____.
15. One of the worst mistakes a parent can make is to _____.
16. If my son or daughter was sick, he or she would feel better if _____.
17. The main reason my spouse or ex-spouse is wanting custody of our child or children is because _____.

9. COMPLETION FORM FOR LITIGANTS (2)

1. If my child was physically fighting with another child, I would _____.
2. If my child began shouting profanities directed at me, I would _____.
3. If my child had a temper tantrum in a grocery store, I would _____.
4. A child's behavior I would have difficulty dealing with would be _____.
5. If I discovered my child (four years old) taking a piece of bubblegum out of the store without my knowledge, I would _____.
6. If my child began making fun of another person, I would _____.
7. If my child accidentally broke a neighbor's window with a baseball, I would __.
8. Typical stages of child development include the:

    "_____" twos.   "_____" fours.

    "_____" threes.   "_____" fives.

9. Typical behavior of a two-year old is _____.
10. An infant needs to learn _____.
11. If my child had a temperature of 102 degrees, I would _____.
12. If a babysitter was with my child for the evening, I would be certain _____.
13. I would like to take my child _____.
14. The usual amount of time I spend with my child each day in recreational or educational activities is _____.
15. It is necessary to attend school activities _____.
16. The appropriate age to teach a child sex education is _____.
17. One of the most recent problem areas any parent needs to be educated about is _____.

10. COMPLETION FORM FOR LITIGANTS (3)

1. I would describe my relationship with my parents as being _____.
2. The main method of discipline my parents used when I was a child was _____.
3. The most traumatic event in my life that I have had to deal with so far is _____.
4. The happiest event in my life so far was _____.
5. The main qualities that attracted me to my spouse or ex-spouse were _____.
6. The main problems in my marriage were _____.
7. I would describe my spouse or ex-spouse as being _____.
8. The most upset I have ever been with my child or children was _____.
9. The main disagreement I would have with my spouse or ex-spouse about child care would be _____.
10. The usual amount of time I spend directly in activities with my child each day is _____.
11. If I found out a teenage child of mine got drunk, I would _____.
12. One of the most valuable lessons any person can learn is _____.
13. A quality I really admire is _____.
14. My child probably would say that what he or she likes best about me is _____.
15. My child would probably say that what he or she likes least about me is _____.
16. My child would probably say that what he or she likes best about my spouse or ex-spouse is _____.
17. My child would probably say that what he or she likes least about my spouse or ex-spouse is _____.

11. COMPLETION FORM FOR LITIGANTS (4)

1. The main rules or expectations I have for children are the following: _____.
2. My spouse or ex-spouse's four best qualities are _____
_____.
3. I would like to be remembered as _____.
4. The biggest mistake I ever made was _____.
5. If my child wanted to visit my spouse or ex-spouse on a holiday not specified in the court order, I would _____
_____.
6. I would describe my child's relationship with my spouse or ex-spouse as ____.
7. The most serious trouble I have ever been in is _____
_____.
8. Three of the best gifts any person could ever receive are: _____.
9. A typical day when I am with my child or children would include _____.
10. If I got paid a salary for taking care of my child, I would expect to get paid __.
11. My best parenting skills include _____.
12. If a book was written about my life, it should be entitled _____.
13. My child's preference is to live with _____.
14. When I talk about my spouse or ex-spouse in front of my child, I usually make _____ comments.
15. If my child needed to be in the hospital and only one parent could be in the room, _____ would be my child's choice.
16. If I could have one dream come true, it would be _____
_____.
17. Since court action was initiated, my child has lived with _____.

12. FORM FOR LITIGANTS

Please circle any item below which either currently or in the past pertains directly to you, one of your children, your spouse or ex-spouse, a relative, or any person who is currently a member of your household.

1. Alcoholism
2. Drug addiction
3. Mental illness
4. Any disease diagnosed to be terminal
5. AIDS
6. Has physically or sexually abused a child (determined by Department of Children and Family Services investigation)
7. Neglected a child (determined by Department of Children and Family Services investigation)

13. COMPLETION FORM FOR CHILDREN (1)

Please complete any questions that you can complete without any difficulty. *Please sign your name and put today's date on each form you complete.*

1. If I was stranded on an island, I would feel best if I was rescued by _____.
2. If I wanted to have friends stay at my house for a few days _____ would be the most accepting of my friends visiting.
3. If my dad ever got any kind of award, it would probably be for _____.
4. If my mom ever got any kind of award, it would probably be for _____.
5. My mom and dad used to have most of their arguments about _____.
6. The parent that spends more time in activities with me is _____.
7. The parent that seems the most negative about the other parent is _____.
8. The parent I have spent the most time with since I was born is _____.
9. The parent that would be the most likely to take me to a museum or an educational program is _____.
10. If I wanted to visit one of my parents at a time that wasn't a scheduled visit, the parent that would be the most willing for me to visit the other parent would be _____.
11. If I wanted to go to a movie and both my parents had other plans, _____ would be the most willing to change plans to go with me.
12. If I were the judge, I would decide that _____ would be the best parent to have permanent custody of me and/or other children.
13. The main reason my mom wants custody is _____.
14. The main reason my dad wants custody is _____.
15. The parent that seems to consider my ideas and feelings the most is _____.
16. The parent who has qualities that I would most like to have myself is _____.
17. The parent I feel most relaxed with the majority of the time is _____.

14. COMPLETION FORM FOR CHILDREN (2)

Please complete all the questions below that you can complete without any difficulty.

1. My mom often says that dad _____.
2. My dad often says that mom _____.
3. The parent that helps me most with homework is _____.
4. A book written about my mom should be called _____.
5. A book written about my dad should be called _____.
6. I like to be treated like _____ treats me.
7. Dad places the most importance on _____.
8. Mom places the most importance on _____.
9. _____ has the most patience with me.
10. _____ talks to me the most about topics I am interested in.
11. I would rather spend holidays with _____.
12. _____ is more willing to take me places that I enjoy the most.
13. My dad's best quality is _____.
14. My mom's best quality is _____.
15. The parent that makes me feel the most special and worthwhile is _____.
16. The parent that says the most negative statements in general is _____.
17. The saddest I have ever been is _____
_____.

15. COMPLETION FORM FOR CHILDREN (3)

Please complete each sentence with the first ideas that come to your mind.

1. The famous person my dad reminds me of is _____
_____.

2. The famous person my mom reminds me of is _____
_____.

3. I am happiest when _____
_____.

4. I am saddest when _____
_____.

5. My mom becomes the most angry when _____
_____.

6. My dad becomes the most angry when _____
_____.

7. If I could change one thing about my dad, it would be _____
_____.

8. If I could change one thing about my mom, it would be _____
_____.

9. If I was in the hospital and only one parent could stay in the room with me, I would choose _____ to be with me.

10. If I could go to any place I chose for a day (such as to the amusement park) and I could only take one of my parents, I would want to go with _____.

11. The parent that would be the most willing to help me if I got in trouble would be _____.

12. The happiest time I have had with my mom was _____
_____.

13. The happiest time I have had with my dad was _____
_____.

14. The famous person I like best is _____

15. If I had $100.00, I would _____
_____.

16. I am really looking forward to the day when _____
_____.

17. When I get out of school, I would like to _____
_____.

16. COMPLETION FORM FOR CHILDREN (4)

Please complete each sentence with the first ideas that come to your mind.

1. If I won $500.00, I would want to _____.
2. If I feel real sad, I would feel better talking to _____
   _____.
3. My dad and I enjoy _____.
4. My mom and I enjoy _____.
5. If I got into trouble, I would want to talk to _____.
6. If I had a big secret, I would feel more comfortable discussing it with _____.
7. It would be easier to deal with my parent's divorce if mom would _____.
8. It would be easier to deal with my parent's divorce if dad would _____.
9. I feel under the most pressure regarding the custody issue when _____.
10. If I felt unhappy, I would want to be with _____.
11. What I like best about my mom is _____.
12. What I like best about my dad is _____.
13. My happiest times are _____.
14. My friends have the most fun with me when _____
    _____
15. The most fun I have ever had was _____.
16. If I was sick, I would want to be with _____.
17. The person that makes me feel the most worthwhile and important is _____.

17. TRUE-FALSE FORM FOR CHILDREN

Please circle the answer (T for true or F for False) that is the most correct.

T F 1. I have had a bruise, mark or other injury as a result of discipline.
T F 2. I have been touched in places that made me feel uncomfortable.
T F 3. My mom usually doesn't say anything positive about my dad.
T F 4. My dad usually doesn't say anything positive about my mom.
T F 5. My dad would be happier if I didn't want to spend time with mom.
T F 6. My mom would be happier if I didn't want to spend time with dad.
T F 7. I feel under the most pressure when I'm with my dad.
T F 8. I feel under the most pressure when I'm with my mom.
T F 9. My dad asks a lot of questions about my visits with mom.
T F 10. My mom asks a lot of questions about my visits with dad.
T F 11. My dad should be given custody by the judge.
T F 12. My mom should be given custody by the judge.
T F 13. I have thought at times that life is not worth living.
T F 14. My mom has a problem with drinking alcoholic beverages.
T F 15. My dad has a problem with drinking alcoholic beverages.
T F 16. My dad has hit me in places other than on my buttock area.
T F 17. My mom has hit me in places other than on my buttock area.

18. ADDITIONAL QUESTIONS TO UTILIZE IN INTERVIEWING CHILDREN

Please respond to those questions which apply to your situation. If your answer includes more than one person, please indicate.

1. Who prepares your meals?
2. Who usually selects your clothes?
3. Who enrolls you in school?
4. Who takes you to the doctor for appointments?
5. Who takes you to the dentist?
6. Who attends school functions such as an open house at school?
7. Who usually takes care of you when you are sick?
8. Who takes you to get your hair cut?
9. Who takes your temperature when you are sick?
10. Who gives you medicine when it is needed?
11. Who helps you with your homework?
12. Who plays with you most of the time?
13. Who takes you to day care or school?
14. Who talks to you if you have questions or want to talk about daily activities?
15. If you had to be in the hospital for a few days and only one person could be with you in your room, who would you choose to be with you and why?
16. Who usually disciplines you when needed?
17. Who supervises your daily activities (including your (17a) personal hygiene, (17b) your recreational activities, (17c) your assigned tasks around the house, (17d) school assignments, and (17e) other daily activities).

19. ADDITIONAL QUESTIONS FOR LITIGANTS IN CUSTODY CASES

1. If you obtain legal custody of your child or children and the child wants to write and/or call the other parent, would you have any objections? Would there be any limit on frequency of calls or letters? Please give reason for your answers.
2. If your ex-spouse refuses to pay court-ordered child support payments but your child benefits from visiting your ex-spouse, would you object to the visits being continued? Please give reason for your answer.
3. If your child wants to visit your ex-spouse at times longer than the court order specifies, would you have any objections? Please explain reason for your answer.
4. If your ex-spouse obtains legal custody of the child or children and in the future your child does not want to visit you as often as the court order specifies, what would be your reaction?
5. Do you have any concerns about your ex-spouse's parenting abilities? If so, what are your concerns?
5a. Does your ex-spouse have any problems that would interfere with his ability to assume parental responsibilities for a child on a permanent basis? If answer is yes, please explain giving specific facts to substantiate.
6. Do you and your ex-spouse disagree on any child care issues? If so, what are they and what is the nature of your disagreement?
7. If you could only take one paid vacation day within the next month and you had a chance to participate in the activity of your choice (with or without your child or children present) what would you choose to spend the day doing and why? Would your children be with you or would they be with someone else (such as a responsible relative or babysitter?)

20. STATEMENT OF UNDERSTANDING REGARDING CONFIDENTIALITY

I understand that there is *no* guarantee that any information I give in interviews or answers I give on forms will be kept confidential. The forms I complete will not be shown directly to other family members by the investigator; however, any attorney or judge involved in this case may request to see the investigator's file, and any request of this nature will be honored.

I also understand that the investigator may be requested to testify at a court hearing in which case any information in the investigator's file, information obtained during the investigation, or information on forms may be revealed during testimony.

_____
Signature of Litigant or Child
(if child is old enough to sign his or her name)

_____
(Date)

_____
Signature of Witness

_____
(Date)

21. FORM LETTER TO SEND TO SCHOOL IF SCHOOL AGE CHILDREN

Date
Re: _____

(Address)

Dear

Our agency has been ordered by the _____ County Court to complete a custody investigation in regard to _____. An important part of our investigation is obtaining a report on each child's progress in school of all school-age children involved in custody litigation.

I would appreciate it if the enclosed form could be completed by the person at school who has the most first-hand information regarding the above-named child. Please return the completed form in the enclosed self-addressed, stamped envelope at your earliest convenience.

Thank you for your cooperation in this regard.

Very truly yours,

Mary E. Lindley, MSW, CSW

MEL:ds

enclosure

Date mailed:

22. SCHOOL REPORT FORM TO BE UTILIZED IN CUSTODY INVESTIGATIONS

Name of Child _____

Child's Birthdate _____

Child's Parents or Parent Substitute _____

Child's Address _____

Grade in School _____

Name of School _____

Address of School _____

Telephone Number of School _____

Please indicate the current academic functioning of the above child.

Is child working up to his potential at the present time? If answer is no, please list reasons if known.

Please summarize child's appearance including personal hygiene. Is child currently exhibiting any behavior problems? If so, please describe the problems and include any specific relevant information.

Has child ever been absent or tardy for reasons other than reasons considered acceptable by school staff? If answer is yes, please indicate number of times during this school year child has been absent or tardy and reasons, if known.

Appendices

Please summarize child's adjustment socially.

Have school staff been contacted by any family member regarding the child's progress in school? If answer is yes, please specify who has contacted school staff, frequency of contacts, and the nature of the contacts.

Do you know if any family member helps the above-named child with school work? If answer is yes, please specify name of person that helps with work and the reason you believe child receives help from person listed.

Have school staff ever initiated contacts with a relative of child that resulted in no response? If so, please explain in some detail.

Does child ever discuss his home situation? If so, please summarize any relevant information concerning child's home situation.

Does child ever express a preference regarding where he would like to live on a permanent basis? If answer is yes, please specify the child's stated preference and reasons, if known.

_____
(signature of person completing form)

_____
(title of person completing form)

_____
(date form completed)

23. LAW ENFORCEMENT FORM

Re: _____ Custody
Litigants: _____
DOB: _____

_____
DOB: _____

Our agency has been ordered by _____ County Court to complete a Custody Investigation regarding the above-named litigants. An important part of this investigation is to obtain verification of whether or not each litigant has had any involvement with the law enforcement officials in terms of charges or court convictions. Please complete this form and return the completed form in the enclosed self-addressed envelope at your earliest convenience. Please note the litigant's signed authorization at the bottom of this form acknowledging their consent for you to provide requested information.

I want to thank you in advance for your cooperation.

1. Has above named litigant ever had charges filed against him or her? _____
   If answer is yes, please list specific charges, appropriate dates and the outcome of each charge (if known).

   _____
   _____
   _____
   _____

2. Have there been any court convictions regarding the above-named litigant? _____ If answer is yes, please list specific court convictions including appropriate dates.

   _____
   _____
   _____
   _____

3. Has the above-named litigant or any relative of the litigant ever been involved in any criminal behavior directly related to children? If answer is yes, please explain.

_____

_____

_____

_____

| Date | Signature of Person Completing Form |

I authorize verification of the above information as part of the Custody Investigation.

| Date | Signature of Litigant |

| Date | Signature of Witness |

24. COLLATERAL FORM

Re: _____ Custody
Litigants: _____
_____

Our agency has been ordered by the _____ Circuit Court to complete a custody investigation regarding the above-named litigants. An important part of this investigation is to obtain relevant first-hand observations of collaterals.

Please answer the following questions that you could answer based on facts (such as your own personal observations of the above litigant's interactions with the child or children involved in the above named contested custody case).

Please return your completed form in the enclosed self-addressed envelope. The returned forms completed by collaterals are *not* submitted with my report to the court, but the information is beneficial in trying to obtain as complete a picture as possible regarding the parenting abilities of the litigants.

Please attached additional sheets of paper if necessary to relate your observations.

In answering each question please specify the name of the litigant you are relating observations about so it is clear which facts pertain to which litigant.

I want to thank you in advance for your cooperation in sharing any relevant observations or other facts you have that pertain to this particular custody case. *Be certain that you list facts to substantiate your answer to each question you respond to.*

1. Do you know only one or both litigants involved in this case? _____ M F
2. Are you related to either one of the litigants? _____ If the answer is yes, please indicate which litigant you are related to and the nature of your relationship with that person. _____
3. Have you had opportunities to observe one or both litigant's interaction with their child or children? _____. If answer is yes, please summarize your observations in regard to each litigant. _____

_____

_____

_____

_____

4. Please summarize each litigant's parental strengths. _____

   _____
   _____
   _____
   _____
   _____

5. Please summarize each litigant's parental weaknesses. _____

   _____
   _____
   _____
   _____
   _____

6. Do you have any knowledge of either litigant having any problem that would interfere with his or her ability to assume parental responsibilities on a permanent basis? _____ If answer is yes, please specify facts to substantiate this.

   _____
   _____
   _____
   _____
   _____

7. Do you have any facts or observations to substantiate any of the following? If answer is yes, please summarize facts relating to each question and answer that you personally are able to substantiate.
   A. Which litigant has spent the greatest amount of time in assuming responsibilities for child care tasks? _____

   _____

B. Which litigant has spent more time in recreational activities with the child or children? _____

C. Which litigant has provided more educational opportunities for the child or children or provides better quality care? _____

D. Which litigant is better able to focus on the needs of children? _____

E. Which litigant has provided the most daily care of the child or children since the litigant's separation? _____

_____

_____

_____

_____

_____

F. Which litigant seems to be more willing to encourage a positive relationship between his spouse or ex-spouse and child? _____

_____

_____

_____

_____

_____

G. Which litigant would provide the best role model for a child? _____

_____

_____

_____

_____

_____   _____
         Date   Signature of Person Completing Form

(Please do not forget to sign your name on the appropriate line above and indicate the date you completed the form).

25. VERIFICATION OF EMPLOYMENT FORM

Re: _____ Custody
Litigants: _____
_____

Our agency has been ordered by the _____ County Court to complete a Custody Investigation regarding the above-named litigants. An important part of this Investigation is to obtain verification of employment. Please complete this form as it relates to the above-named litigants and return the completed form in the enclosed self-addressed envelope at your earliest convenience.

Please note litigant's signed authorization at the bottom of this form acknowledging consent for you to provide requested information.

1. Job title of litigant, if still currently employed by you. _____
2. Date current employment began: _____.
3. Amount of gross monthly salary: _____.
4. Hours of employment: _____.
5. Please indicate if there are any problems regarding job performance. _____

_____

_____

_____

_____   _____
    Date   Signature of Person Completing Form

I authorize verification of the above information as part of the Custody Investigation.

_____   _____
    Date   Signature of Litigant

_____   _____
    Date   Signature of Witness

26. SAMPLE, NON-BINDING PARENTAL AGREEMENT

Custody and Visitation Agreement between John and Jane Doe

The following agreement was made between John and Jane Doe at the office of Dr. Gordon Plumb on January 1, 1989. Both John Doe and Jane Doe are aware that this agreement is nonbinding until they have met with attorneys and their attorneys draw up a legally binding agreement and they both sign such an agreement.

This agreement was made by both parties within the spirit of the following guidelines.
1. That both parents share a love and desire for (list children).
2. That in order to perform their various parental duties and privileges they need to parent their children in a high quality/low conflict manner.
3. That their children are at risk of developing emotional and/or psychophysiological damage should they place their children in loyalty conflicts.
4. That children develop optimally when they feel secure with each parent and their energy is not used to defend one or the other parent in an attempt to take care of their feelings. Parents are there to take care of children's feelings, not children the parents' feelings.
5. That part of the security children need is to know where and with whom they are living most of the time.
6. That children change and develop over time. With these changes the parents need to remain flexible and make appropriate changes in custody/visitation. That child mental health experts are available and preferable to litigation for the resolution of such developmental problems in the future.

Physical Custody:

It is agreed that Martha (10) and Joel (8) physically reside with Mrs. Doe in their current home.

Responsibility:

Mrs. Doe will be responsible for the day-to-day care of both children while they are residing with her. Major decisions or events involving the children will be shared with Mr. Doe. Examples of major decisions include health care, counseling, educational options, special schools, summer camps or plans, etc.

Examples of major events include school functions, sports or activities functions, graduations, awards ceremonies, etc.

Visitation:

1. The children will visit with Mr. Doe together every other weekend from Friday at approximately 6:00 PM until Sunday at 6:00 PM commencing Friday, January 6, 1989. Mr. Doe will be responsible for pick up and delivery of the children.
2. Mr. Doe will have dinner with Martha on every Wednesday that his schedule allows and return her home by 8:00 PM.
3. Mr. Doe will have dinner with Joel every Thursday that his schedule allows and return him home by 8:00 PM.
4. In addition to every other weekend with both children, Mr. Doe will have Martha and Joel separately for a weekend once every two months commencing on January 27th with Martha and February 24th with Joel. Martha's second alone visit with her father will be March 24th. Joel's second alone visit will be April 21. The parents recognize that there may be overlapping visits at some point in the future and they agree to be flexible in fulfilling the spirit of the every other month alone visitation by adjusting the regular schedule when necessary.
5. Both children will spend every other major holiday with their father beginning with Easter, 1989. Major holidays are Easter, Memorial Day, July 4th, Labor Day, Thanksgiving and Christmas. On Thanksgiving, Christmas and each of the children's birthdays, the children will spend at least three hours with the parent who does not have the children during that holiday.
6. The parents agree to be flexible when any special events occur and the children would miss out if the regular visitation schedule would be followed. In general, however, special events should be planned in accordance with the visitation schedule.
7. During summer vacations each parent will inform the other of vacation plans that include the children so that the children can have the benefit of vacation with each parent. Mr. Doe will have the children for two separate two-week periods between June 1st and August 20th. Mr. Doe's vacation plans with the children are included in the four week total.
8. The parents agree that should disputes arise concerning the children which they are not able to resolve themselves, they will seek the services of an appropriate child mental health expert in an attempt to mediate or arbitrate the problem.

This concludes the parental agreement. I assume that my services will no longer be required unless I am contacted by one or both of the attorneys. It has been a pleasure to assist Mr. and Mrs. Doe in a nonadversarial resolution of their custody dilemma. If I can be of further service, please contact me.

Sincerely yours,

GP/cam

Gordon Plumb, Ph.D.
Registered Psychologist

27. SAMPLE INVESTIGATIVE CUSTODY REPORT

Sue Sun vs. Sam Sun

Cause No: 77-777-77
                 Jasper County Court

Children: Stan Sun
Born: 2-27-78
               Steve Sun
Born: 7-27-80

Mother: Sue Sun
               17 Seventh Street
               Newton, Illinois 62448

Father: Sam Sun
               1707 Seventh Street
               Newton, Illinois 62448

This report is submitted in accordance with an Order of the Court to investigate both parties relative to the custody of one minor child (Stan). To this worker's knowledge, the date for the final hearing in this matter is set for July 17, 1988.

RELEVANT BACKGROUND:

Stan and Sue Sun were divorced in September, 1980, soon after the birth of their second son, Steve. They have one additional child, Stan (date of birth: 2/27/78) who is the primary focus of this social investigation. Sue Sun was granted custody of both children at the 1980 divorce; however, Sam Sun actually has had physical custody of Stan since 1980. Sue Sun states that she felt overburdened with responsibility and stress at that time, especially having a new baby just before a divorce; consequently she allowed Stan to live with his father until she felt better able to handle two children. Since February, 1980, Stan has resided with Sam Sun and visited his mother. Steve Sun has resided with Sue Sun and has had visitation with his father. In March, 1985, Sue Sun remarried, but this did not alter the childcare arrangements. In November of 1987 Sam remarried. In January, 1988, Sue Sun filed for custody of Stan. In January, 1988, the Cumbersome County Court ordered a custody investigation. This examiner was then appointed to do said examination.

I. METHOD UTILIZED:

The custody investigation procedures included the following: each litigant's completing a questionnaire with social history information, investigator's conducting home visits, interviews with child or children involved in custody issues if child is five years old or older; investigator observing each litigant with the child or children; litigant's completion of forms; child's completion of forms if old enough to complete forms or to be interviewed regarding the questions on the forms; collaterals with relevant information were contacted.

Sue and Sam each completed a set of forms that this investigator designed to help in assessing parenting abilities of the litigants, the needs of the children and the Major and Minor criteria considered to be important in the custody investigation. The forms completed by Sue and Sam were in addition to the basic data sheet and completed by each of them, a copy of which is attached to this report. A school report on each child is also attached to this report. All procedures were followed with the goal of the children's welfare being the primary consideration.

II. CONTACTS WITH LITIGANTS: (Including contacts with Stan and Steve).

6/7/88: In-person interview with Sue Sun at her home.

6/7/88: In-person interview with Stan Sun at Newton Consolidated Grade School in Newton, Illinois.

6/17/88: In-person interview with Sam Sun at his home; Susie was also present during this interview.

6/17/88: In-person interview with Steven Sun at Newton Consolidated Grade School in Newton, Illinois.

6/17/88: Observation of Sue, Sam and Steve at the park in Newton, Illinois; this particular scheduled visitation lasted approximately 40 minutes.

Total number of contact hours: 12   Total number of hours: 17

III. CONTACTS WITH COLLATERALS:

This social worker did talk with the principal of Newton Grade School as well as with Steve's and Stan's teachers, Tom D. and Jon P. As indicated previously, school forms were obtained on both Stan and Steve. Due to time constraints, additional collaterals were not interviewed.

IV. OBSERVATIONS DURING VISITS TO THE HOMES OF SUE AND SAM:

Sue's home was clean, neat, and adequately furnished. Stan and Steve share a bedroom with bunk beds. Sue's stepson has a bedroom of his own, and Sue and her husband have the third bedroom.

Sam's house was neat, clean, and adequately furnished. Sam's home has two bedrooms and Stan and Steve share one of the bedrooms.

According to employers, Sam Sun's combined income is approximately $28,000 per year. Sue Sun's combined income is approximately $32,000 per year.

V. FORMS UTILIZED:

Standard forms and questionnaires were filled out by both parents separately with no assistance by any third party. Significant questions and responses by each parent follow:

Sue's answers to some of the questions include the following:

If I had a choice, I would not permit my child or children to visit the other parent. —TRUE

If my spouse or ex-spouse did not have so many faults, our marriage would have been successful. —TRUE

If a child cannot live with both parents, it is important that they take sides and express their preferences to both parents so that it is clear where the child's loyalties lie. —TRUE

If your child lives with you for several years and you have legal custody and later your child expresses a desire to live with the noncustodial parent, the child's wish should not be given serious consideration. —TRUE

I find it difficult to say anything positive about my spouse or ex-spouse. —TRUE

I would be happier if my spouse or ex-spouse would be denied any visitation rights. —TRUE

I try to get detailed information about my spouse or ex-spouse from my child after each visit my child has with my spouse or ex-spouse. —TRUE

Children have a responsibility to meet the needs of their parents. —TRUE

I am happier when my child does not enjoy being with my spouse or ex-spouse. —TRUE

I became most angry when Sam permitted Stan to wear his hair spiked.

I am sad whenever the kids go to Sam's.

The most frustrating part of being a parent is being bothered by the boys' dad.

My spouse's or ex-spouse's greatest fault is being filthy and having a terrible personality.

If I could have just one wish, it would be to have my boys without being bothered by their dad.

The most frustrating age of a child to cope with is age 13 because they want to go places without me.

I can be pleased with the job I have done as a parent if Sam would leave me alone.

I would describe my spouse or ex-spouse as being a bad influence.

The main disagreement I would have with my spouse or ex-spouse about child care would be he doesn't keep the house clean or practice good personal hygiene.

The biggest mistake I ever made was marrying Sam.

I would describe my child's relationship with my spouse or ex-spouse as terrible.

Sam's answers to some of the questions include the following:

If my spouse or ex-spouse did not have so many faults, our marriage would have been successful. — FALSE

If a child cannot live with both parents, it is important that they take sides and express their preference to both parents so that it is clear where the child's loyalties lie. — FALSE

If your child lives with you for several years and you have legal custody and later on your child expresses a desire to live with the noncustodial parent, the child's wish should not be given serious consideration. — FALSE

Children should not express their ideas or opinions on important issues concerning them. — FALSE

I find it difficult to say anything positive about my spouse or ex-spouse. — FALSE

I would be happier if my spouse or ex-spouse would be denied any visitation rights. — FALSE

I try to get detailed information about my spouse or ex-spouse from my child after each visit my child has with my spouse or ex-spouse. — FALSE

If my child refused to visit my spouse or ex-spouse, I would permit my child to not visit even if I did not know any legitimate reason for my child's refusing to visit. — FALSE

Children have a responsibility to meet the needs of their parents. — FALSE

I am happier when my child does not enjoy being with my spouse or ex-spouse. — FALSE

I become the most angry when people mistreat my sons.

I am sad whenever I see families split up and the children hurt inside because they love and they get hurt for loving.

It definitely is being abusive to a child if a person fights over children and pulls them one way and the other saying negative things about the other parent.

If I could have just one wish, it would be to erase all the memories of the contested custody.

The most difficult part about a divorce and/or contested custody situation is the children — when they love both parents such as in this case.

The main problems in my marriage were my disabilities.

I would describe my spouse or ex-spouse as being loving and warm most of the time.

The main disagreement I would have with my spouse or ex-spouse about child care would be using them against one another and others when she is mad.

My child probably would say that what he or she likes best about me is I'm sober and don't drink anymore.

My child would probably say that what he or she likes least about me is I used to drink.

The biggest mistake I ever made was taking that first drink.

If my child wanted to visit my spouse or ex-spouse on a holiday not specified in the court order, I would let them go.

My child's preference is to live with both parents.

When I talk about my spouse or ex-spouse in front of my child, I usually <u>make favorable comments</u>.

VI. OBSERVATIONS OF SAM, SUE, STAN AND STEVE AT NEWTON PARK ON JUNE 17, 1988:

In general, both children related well with both parents. Sam played ball with Steve and Stan separately. Sue played ball with Steve and Stan separately. In general, both Steve and Stan played separately. Stan was affectionate with his dad. Steve was affectionate with his mom. During the observation period, Steve spontaneously mentioned that possibly when the court hearing is over, he will be able to start getting to spend whole weekends with his dad, and that he is real hopeful he can start spending more time with his dad.

In observing both Stan and Steve on this particular date, both boys had on shorts, gym shoes, socks and a shirt and both appeared neat and clean in appearance. There was no noticeable difference in personal hygiene or the type of clothing worn by either child.

VII. GENERAL OBSERVATIONS AND CONCLUSIONS:

Since this social worker's understanding is that the primary custody issue is in regard to Stan, the following conclusions are focused primarily as they relate to Stan.

1. There is genuine mutual love and affection between both parents and their sons.
2. Steve would like to visit his dad more frequently than is currently being permitted by his mother.
3. Steve would like his visits with his dad to be of longer duration than they currently are.
4. It seems evident that Sam Sun individualizes the needs of children and is more child-oriented than Sue. In interviews as well as answers to forms completed, Sam demonstrates a deep concern for the feelings and needs of his sons; in contrast, Sue primarily focuses on superficial concerns such as Stan's hair cut, clothes that he wears, or cleanliness of the house.
5. Stan indicated that his preference is to live with his mother but there is reason to believe that his stated preference may not be his true preference, but instead may be a reflection of his not wanting to alienate his mother. In my professional assessment, Stan feels very secure in his relationship with his dad but understandably would be confused by his mother's permitting him to live with his dad since 1980 until February of this year and now all of a sudden mother is

strongly opposing his living with his dad. Stan may have a fear of losing his mother's love if he does not express a preference for her.

In comparing Stan's stated preference for living with his mother (e.g., "She said she would give me $10 a week allowance.") with Stan's response on the children's questionnaires, there is a striking inconsistency. On the questionnaires it appears that Stan feels more secure with his father. A few examples of Stan's written responses follow:

- If I wanted to have friends stay at my house for a few days <u>DAD</u> would be most accepting of my friend's visiting.
- If I wanted to visit one of my parents at a time that wasn't a scheduled visit, the parent that would be the most willing for me to visit the other parent would be <u>DAD</u>.
- The parent that makes me feel the most special and worthwhile is <u>DAD</u>.
- If I were in the hospital and only one parent could stay in the room with me, I would choose <u>DAD</u> to be with me.

6. Sam was much more open and honest in discussing problem areas than Sue and without any hesitation acknowledged his past mistakes.
7. Sam (by his own admission) had serious problems the first few years that Stan lived with him, such as alcohol and drug abuse, which would have posed legitimate concerns that could have easily justified Sue's removal of Stan from Sam's home or her not permitting Stan initially to live with his father. Sue was aware of the problems, had legal custody of Stan, and willingly left Stan with his dad when Stan was of preschool age at a time when the potential for Stan's being at risk of harm would certainly be greater than at his current age, nine. Legitimate reasons that would warrant removal of Stan from Sam's home would have been present several years ago rather than at the present time.
8. Stan reports a lot of positive changes in his life recently, especially his remarriage. Sue made the decision to try and get custody of Stan a short time after this marriage with no other apparent motivational variables.
9. Sue clearly focuses more on Stan's weaknesses than her own. She has problems in coping with his behavior (undefined and/or unsubstantiated) and clearly believes that Stan has current problems which need correcting (problems which she blames on Sam's influence). In general, Sue is very critical of Stan.
10. Sam focused on Stan's strengths, had difficulty thinking of anything negative to say about Stan, and indicated that Stan is well behaved with him.
11. Stan and Steve do not seem to be close emotionally, they have lived apart since 1980 essentially and it would *not* seem to be detrimental if they continued to live in separate homes.
12. It would be beneficial to Stan and Steve if Sue and Sam could work cooperatively together with their new spouses in focusing on the needs of the children.
13. Both Stan and Steve could benefit from both parents and stepparents being active participants in their lives.
14. Stan feels under pressure emotionally (regarding the custody issues) when he is with his dad as well as when he is with his mom.
15. It is evident that Stan and Steve love both parents very deeply and have positive feelings about both stepparents (Susie and George).

VIII INVESTIGATORS' CONCLUSIONS AS TO THE MAJOR AND MINOR CRITERIA FOR CUSTODY:

Major Criteria:

1. *Psychological Parent:* Sam Sun appears to be more of a psychological parent to Stan than Sue Sun. Both parents love their children; however, Sam seems to show more of the qualities of a positive, psychological parent, including the children's needs to have a healthy relationship to both parents. Sam has had the primary caretaking responsibilities for all of Stan's life and it is consistent that their bond to each other is stronger than Stan's bond with his mother.
2. *Continuity of Relationship:* Sam has been the primary custodial parent of Stan since 1980.
3. *Emotional Stability:* Both parents appear to be emotionally stable. Sam's problems with alcohol and drugs during the first couple of years with Stan have been eliminated and Sam has lived a responsible lifestyle with no drug or alcohol problems since 1984. Sam appears nondefensive and insightful about his past irresponsibilities. Sam shows more evidence of understanding Stan's needs than does Sue. Refer to evaluator's report for more information on this category.
4. *Continuity of Sibling Relationship:* This criterion would be met if Sue Sun was awarded custody of Stan. However, the brothers have lived apart for approximately eight years and have adjusted well to the situation. There appears to be no significant risk to the boys remaining in separate households, especially if the relationship between their parents becomes cooperative and supportive.
5. *Parental Flexibility:* This criterion clearly favors Sam. He is genuinely aware of the need for both boys to have a conflict-free relationship with their mother. Both on her questionnaire and in person, Sue maintained a chronically negative attitude toward Sam which will make it extremely difficult for the boys to have a conflict-free relationship with both their mother and father.
6. *Physical Health:* Both parents appear to be in good health.

Minor Criteria:

1. *Parent's Moral Character:* Both parents appear to be of good moral character. Sam's alcohol and drug problems of the past along with some irresponsible parenting appear to be resolved.
2. *Parent's Financial, Material and Cultural Assets:* There appears to be no significant differences in these areas among the parents.
3. *Favoring a Two-Parent Home:* Both Sam and Sue have remarried and currently have stable married lives.
4. *Favoring the Genuine Wishes of the Child:* The expressed wish of Stan is to be with his mother. A ten year old's preference should be given some consideration;

however, the judgment of a boy this age is not expected to be motivated by mature consideration. Also, there is some concern on the part of this examiner that Stan's motivation may be more an appeasement of his mother and longing for his mother's love than of a genuine preference for his mother for healthy reasons.

5. *Favoring Child's Access to Extended Family:* This criterion clearly favors Sam as Sue is vehemently opposed to either child having much to do with Sam. Sue has been blaming of Sam's parents for some of the difficulties in their past marital relationship.

IV: CONCLUSIONS AND RECOMMENDATIONS:

1. That Sam Sun be granted custody of Stan. That joint-custody not be awarded in that Sue Sun lacks the flexibility to have a High Quality-Low Conflict relationship with Stan and Sam.
2. That visitation of Stan be made in accordance with recommendations provided in evaluator's report.
3. That Steve be granted more visitation with Sam for lengthier periods of time in accordance with recommendations by the evaluator.
4. That visitation be granted which includes more time with Stan and Steve together in the same household.
5. That Sue Sun consider counseling to examine her feelings of hostility toward Sam. This could well be important to the future of both parents' relationships with their children as well as to the future of the children's adult relationships.

Mary E. Lindley, M.S.W., C.S.W.

*When there is no evaluator, visitation recommendations should be made explicit in this report.

BIBLIOGRAPHY

1. Gardner, Richard A.: *Child Custody Litigation, A Guide for Parents and Mental Health Professionals,* New Jersey, Creative Therapeutics, 1986.
2. Goldstein, Joseph, Freud, Anna, and Schmit, Albert J.: *Beyond the Best Interests of the Child,* New York, Free Press, 1973.
3. Hodges, William F.: *Intervention for Children of Divorce,* New York, John Wiley, 1986.
4. Lindley, Mary E.: *A Manual on Investigating Child Custody Reports,* Springfield, IL, Charles C Thomas, 1988.
5. Kopp, Sheldon: *The Pickpocket and the Saint,* Toronto, Bantam Books, 1983.
6. Gardner, Richard A.: *The Parental Alienation Syndrome and the Differentiation between Fabricated and Genuine Child Abuse,* New Jersey, Creative Therapeutics, 1987.
7. Franks, Maurice R.: *Winning Custody, A No-Holds-Barred Guide for Fathers,* Englewood Cliffs, NJ, Prentice-Hall, 1983.

INDEX

A

Abuse charges in custody litigation
    advantages Team/evaluator approach to, 77–78
    allegations of, 74–75
        possibilities resulting in, 74–75
    "children never lie" theory, 74
    differentiating bona fide from fabricated, 76–77
        Sex abuse Legitimacy Scale (*see* Sex Abuse Legitimacy Scale)
    factors in investigation of, 75–76
    increased incidence of, 73–74
    with PAS situations, 73–74
Adversarial litigation
    alternative models to, 81–86
        hypothetical model, 81–86
    Children First (see Children First)
    ending adversarial litigation, 79–80

B

Berger, Sanford J., 87

C

Children in custody litigation
    effects change of lifestyle on, 65–66
    social investigator's interviews with child, 37–40
        forms to complete by child, 107, 108, 109, 110, 111, 112
        questions used, 39–40
    visitations (*see* Visitation)
Collaterals in custody litigation
    social investigator's interviews with, 40–42
        form used, sample, 120–123
        questions used, 41–42
Child custody and litigation
    adversarial (*see* Adversarial litigation)
    attitudes society toward, 79–80
        adversarial system, 79–80
        fathers as automatic custodians, 79
        parental assessment, 79
        raising of male consciousness, 79–80
        sex blind laws, 79
        "tender years presumption," 79
    Children First (see Children First)
    concluding comments, 86–87
    contemporary focus on evaluations & investigations, 4
    criteria for, 13–18 (*see also* Criteria for custody)
    extent of problem, 3–4, 86
    factors in court decisions, 3–4, 79–80
    future of, 79–87 (*see* Adversarial litigation)
    incidence occurrence, 3
    limitation of courts to deal with, 3–4
    maintaining family integrite & power in, 4–5
    psychological dangers of protracted, 7, 80
    social investigation (*see* Social investigation)
Children First
    contents of meetings, 81
    cost for program, 81
    description, 80–81
Confidentiality, statement of understanding regarding, sample, 114
Criteria for custody placement
    continuity of relationship, 16
        advantages of, 16
        age and, 16
    continuity sibling relationship, 17

Criteria for custody placement (*Continued*)
   emotional stability of parents/guardians, 16–17
      evaluation techniques, 16–17
      favoring a two parent home, 19
      favoring child's access to extending family, 20–21
      favoring the genuine wishes of the child, 19–20
   major criteria, 13–18
      assessment of, 45–46
      continuity of relationship, 16
      continuity of sibling relationships, 17
      emotional stability of parents/guardians, 16–17
      parental flexibility, 17–18
      physical health of parent/guardian, 18
      psychological parent, 13–16
      worksheet used, 90–91
   minor criteria for, 18–21
      assessment of, 45–46
      favoring child's access to extended family, 20–21
      favoring genuine wishes of child, 19–20
      favoring two parent home, 19
      parents' financial, material, cultural assets, 19
      parents' moral character, 18–19
      worksheet used, 91
   parental flexibility, 17–18
   parents' financial, material & cultural assets, 19
   parents' moral character, 18–19
   physical health of parent/guardian, 18
   psychological parent (*see* Psychological parent)
   worksheet used, sample, 90–92
Cuneo, Dan, 80
Custody evaluations and investigations
   psychological evaluation (*see* Psychological evaluation)
   social investigation (*see* Social investigation)
   special problems in, 69–78
      Parent Alienation Syndrome (*see* Parent Alienation Syndrome)
      sex and other abuse, 73–78 (*see also* Abuse charges)

D

Divorce
   frequency marriages ending in, 3
   problem of, 3

F

Family's team
   criteria for custody (*see* Criteria for custody)
   difference mediation/arbitration and, 49–50
   ethical principles underlying structure of, 7–11
      importance of, 8
      listing of, 8–10
   hypothetical model for future, 81–86
      areas of concern, 82–83
      description, 81–82
      solutions to cost dilemma, 83–86
   lack of, 11
   meeting with social investigator, 47
   nonbinding parental agreement, 56
      sample of, 125–126
   parent and team meeting, 50–53
      focus of, 52
      length of, 52–53
      topic areas for, 50–52
   parental righteousness, 53–55
   psychological dangers of protracted litigation, 7, 80
   responsibilities of members of, 10–11
      of guardian-ad-litem, 11
      of psychologist or psychiatrist, 10–11
      of social worker, 10
   structure and function of, 10–11
   teams meeting, 50
   verbal and written agreements, 55–56
Formative years, definition, 15
Franks, Maurice R., 136
Freud, Anna, 8, 9, 14, 15, 16, 136

G

Gardner, Richard A., xi, 4, 7, 17, 25, 27, 49, 69, 70, 71, 72, 74, 76, 77, 78, 80, 86, 136
Golden Chain, definition, 53
Goldstein, Joseph, 8, 9, 14, 15, 16, 136

Index

H

Hodges, William F., 19, 58, 61, 62, 63, 136
Home visit by investigator, 44–46
    emphasis of assessment, 44–45

K

Kopp, Sheldon, 54, 136

L

Lindley, Mary E., xii, 115, 135, 136

M

Mediation and arbitration
    definitions, 48
    use of, 48
Minnesota Multiphasic Personality Inventory (MMPI)
    use of in custody decisions, 16–17
    use of in psychological evaluations, 30

P

Parent Alienation Syndrome, 69–73
    and sex-abuse allegations, 73–74
    brainwashing children by mother, 70
    definition, 69
    handling of with parent, 72
    in determination of custody parent, 72–73
    increased in incidence, 69–70
    key symptom of, 71
    reverse symbiosis of, 71
Parental custody agreement, nonbinding
    obtaining, 55–56
    sample form, 125–126
Parental flexibility
    determination of, 17
    use of visitation of child record, 17–18
Parental righteousness
    definition, 53
    handling of, 54–55
    in child custody litigation, 53
Parents as child custody litigants
    attempts to manipulate child, 38–39

Family's Team approach (*see* Family's Team)
    meeting with Family's team, 50–53
    percent divorced couples as, 3
    psychological evaluation (*see* Psychological evaluation)
    psychological parent (*see* Psychological parent)
    social investigation (*see* Social investigation)
    visitation (*see* Visitation)
Plumb, Gordon B., x, xi, 125, 126
Poshard, Glenn, vi, ix, xi, xiii
Psychological evaluation, 23–31
    child care responsibilities form, sample, 97–98
    children's forms to complete, samples, 107, 108, 109, 110, 111, 112
    collateral form, sample, 120–123
    conditions and procedures for, 23
        letter form, sample, 93–94
    court order for, 23
    criteria worksheet use, 31
        sample, 90–92
    evaluators role, 23–24
    guidelines to parents, 24–25
    joint-parental interview
        arrangements for, 23–24
        forms used, 99–112
        importance of, 24
    law enforcement form to complete, 118–119
    litigant's forms to complete, samples, 99, 100, 101, 102, 103, 104, 105, 106, 113
    parental intake form, sample, 95–96
    school's forms to complete, samples, 115, 116–117
    statement of understanding regarding confidentiality, sample, 114
    types joint interviews used, 25–29
        individual child interview, 29
        individual parent interview, 27
        joint parent-child with each parent separately, 28–29
        joint parental interview, 26–27
    uses and misuses of testing, 30–31
    verification of employment form, sample, 124

Psychological parent
    behaviors indicating, 14
    definition, 15
    determination of, 14–15
    early concept of, 13
    summary, 15
    typical regressive behavior of insecure children, 15

R

Ringuette, Gene, 80

S

Schmit, Albert J., 8, 9, 14, 15, 16, 136
Sex Abuse Legitimacy Scale
    description of, 78
    use of, 76–77
Sexual abuse charges (*see* Abuse charges in custody litigation)
Social investigation, 33–48
    assessment major and minor criteria, 45–46
    employment verification, sample form, 124
    forms and procedures, 42
    home visit, 44–46
    information for final report to court, 46–47
    interviewing children, 37–40
        age for, 37
        forms designed for, 107, 108, 109, 110, 111, 112
    interviewing collaterals, 40–42
        form used, sample, 120–123
        questions used with, 41
    interviewing litigants, 35–37
        forms used, samples, 99, 100, 101, 102, 103, 104, 105, 106, 113
        observations during, 37
    litigant's form to complete for, 35
        sample, 106
    meeting with the Team, 47
    obtaining background information, 35
    parental intake form used, 35
        sample, 95–96
    preparation for, 34–35
    procedures with no evaluation, 47–48
    role of investigator, 33–34
    study content, 33–34
    utilization of forms, 43
    written report, 46
        sample report, 127–135

V

Visitation
    effects change of lifestyle, 65–66
    evaluating parents for, 58
    guidelines for by age & development of child, 63–65
    high conflict parenting, 59–60
    high quality parenting, 59
    ideal, 57–58
    judicial dilemma, 58
    low conflict parenting, 60
    low quality parenting, 59
    of grandparents, 65
    problem of, 57
    recommendations for parenting
        high quality, low conflict parenting, 61
        low quality, high conflict parenting, 61–63
    reducing problems due to, 67
    "Santa Claus" effect, 65
    special considerations in, 65–67
    supervised, 66–67